Fundamentals of Angel Investing

Fundamentals of Angel Investing

A Guide to the Principles, Skills and Concepts Every Investor Needs to Succeed

Hambleton Lord
Christopher Mirabile

www.seraf-investor.com

Copyright © 2016 by Seraf LLC

All rights reserved. No part of this publication may be reproduced, distributed, or transmitted in any form or by any means, including photocopying, recording, or other electronic or mechanical methods, without the prior written permission of the publisher, except in the case of brief quotations embodied in critical reviews and certain other noncommercial uses permitted by copyright law. For permission requests, contact the publisher, addressed "Attention: Permissions Coordinator," at the address below.

support@seraf-investor.com

www.seraf-investor.com

Table of Contents

Part One
A Primer for Angel Investors

1. What's the Magic Number?   5
2. How Successful Angel Investors Allocate Assets   11
3. Angel Investing Returns: Research and Reality   17
4. Angel Investing Exits: The Good, the Bad, and the Ugly   21
5. Look Before You Leap: The Importance of Due Diligence   33
6. When Money is Not Enough: Angel Roles and Human Capital   39
7. Thinking About Risk with Angel Investments   45
8. Angel Investing War Stories   49

Part Two
The 4 Critical Skills Every Angel Investor Should Master

9. Rule #1 in Angel Investing - It's All About the Team   55
10. Size Matters… How Big is Your Market?   61
11. Oxygen, Aspirin or Jewelry: Which Makes a Better Investment?   69
12. How to Apply the 3 P's to Selecting Angel Investments   77
13. Staging Capital: Angel Follow-on Theory   83
14. Convertible Notes: Good or Evil?   89
15. Key US Federal Tax Issues for Angel Investors   95
16. Stock Warrants: Sweetening the Deal for Angel Investors   99
17. Demystifying the Internal Rate of Return Measurement   103
18. Early Stage Investment Syndication: Key Issues   107
19. Timing Is Everything: Angel Investing Success   113

Part Three
Understanding Early-Stage Deal Terms

20. Angel Fundamentals: Understanding Equity Deal Terms   121
21. Mapping Key Deal Terms to Key Investor Concerns   127
22. Understanding Equity Deal Terms - Economics   133
23. Understanding Equity Deal Terms - Investor Rights/Protection   141
24. Understanding Equity Deal Terms - Governance, Management & Control 149
25. Understanding Equity Deal Terms - Exits & Liquidity   155
26. Guide to Angel Investing Documents: Preferred Stock Deals   161
27. Guide to Angel Investing Documents: Convertible Debt Deals   173

Part One

Angel 101
A Primer for Angel Investors

Experience is what you get, when you don't get what you want. Fifteen years ago, when I made my first angel investment, I wish I knew then what I know today. As a newly minted angel in 2000, I assumed that angel investing would be easy to jump into and become successful at. I was partially right… it was easy to jump into. Unfortunately, it wasn't that easy to become successful. I've had my share of luck and good outcomes, but I also learned many painful lessons along the way. Many of them would have been easy to avoid, had I understood a few key concepts. For this reason, Seraf Co-Founder Christopher Mirabile and I are determined to help new angels learn from our mistakes and the mistakes of others we have had the opportunity to observe from our perch at the center of a busy angel ecosystem.

The Angel 101 Chapters are based on a course we teach at our angel group, Launchpad Venture Group. We teach this course several times a year for new members of our group. It's a great, interactive two hour session with lots of Q&A from the audience. It's a fun class to teach because Christopher and I feed off each other's energy, tell war stories, and try our best to keep the audience engaged and entertained. What a great way to learn!

We thought the best way to share the learnings and capture the energy of this live class is to break the class into small manageable segments. The layout for each chapter in this book will be a Question and Answer format. In each chapter, we will alternate roles either asking or answering key questions.

Angel 101 is meant to be a course for angels just starting out. We designed the course to focus on important topics, including:

- The basics of building an angel portfolio
- What kind of return can you expect on your investment
- The theory and practice of asset allocation for angel investing
- What should your expectations be for the time it takes to get an exit
- Why it's important to undertake due diligence before investing
- What are the risks that are inherent in early stage companies
- The importance of investing both financial and human capital
- What are some less obvious pitfalls that need to be considered

After reading this section, you should have a sense for what you are getting into as a newly minted angel investor. You should come away with answers to questions such as:

- How many investments will I need to make if I want to build a diversified angel portfolio?
- How much time and energy will I need to invest to become a successful angel?
- If I make an investment before the company has any customers, how long will it take before I make money on the investment?
- Besides writing a check, how can I help an entrepreneur succeed?
- How do I know if I am investing in the next Facebook? (If we knew the answer to this question, we wouldn't be wasting our time writing this book!)

Angel 101 is just the beginning of your educational journey as an angel investor. Once you master these topics, you can dive into the next section, based on our Angel 201 course. So much to read, so little time.

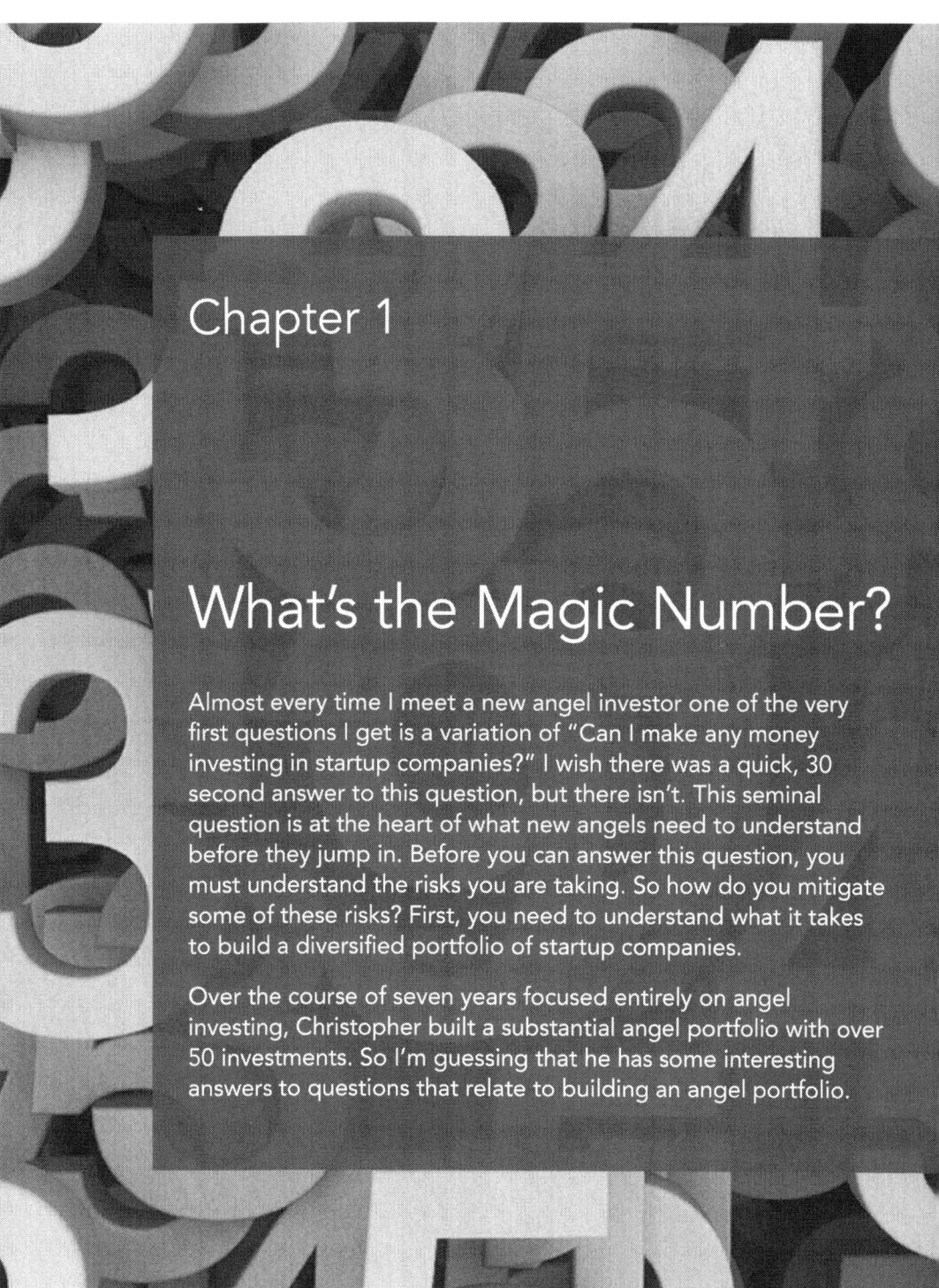

Chapter 1

What's the Magic Number?

Almost every time I meet a new angel investor one of the very first questions I get is a variation of "Can I make any money investing in startup companies?" I wish there was a quick, 30 second answer to this question, but there isn't. This seminal question is at the heart of what new angels need to understand before they jump in. Before you can answer this question, you must understand the risks you are taking. So how do you mitigate some of these risks? First, you need to understand what it takes to build a diversified portfolio of startup companies.

Over the course of seven years focused entirely on angel investing, Christopher built a substantial angel portfolio with over 50 investments. So I'm guessing that he has some interesting answers to questions that relate to building an angel portfolio.

Q

Christopher, think back to 2009 when you started angel investing. Did you have any concept of how many investments you were going to make?

Yes, and no. I had a goal of getting very diversified, and I had a target total amount of capital I wanted to allocate to the angel asset class, and I knew I wanted to focus on first round check sizes in the $10K-25K range. But what I did not know, and could not have known, are three very crucial variables:

- How many companies would merit follow-on investment?
- How much follow-on investment would they require?
- How much returned capital would I have to work with, and how quickly?

Regardless of the target angel allocation, those three variables are going to determine how many companies you can do.

Q

Why did you continue to invest in so many more new companies after you passed that threshold for diversification?

I did not have a specific threshold; the more investments you have, within the bounds of being able to manage them, the better. By manage them, I mean keep on top of them (Seraf helps a lot with that), keep current with their messaging and strategy, help them, have capital available to follow-on and be able to maintain a relationship with the CEO. There is probably an outside limit on the number of companies one can do that with. For a full-time angel such as myself, who is passionate about the space, and energetic about putting in the time, that limit is pretty high - probably in the neighborhood of 50 companies.

Q

Looking into the future, how many companies do you expect to have in your portfolio?

Every portfolio reaches a natural plateau at maturity and the exits begin to off-set the new investments. How many active companies that plateau represents is a function of the pace at which companies are added (particularly good companies - if you have lots of "fast failures," that will bring the numbers down). Here is how the law of plateaus works: if you assume most companies take 5 -10 years to reach an exit, and 50% of your companies fail in their first three years, as the companies in the portfolio age, eventually the rate of harvest will come into approximate equilibrium with the rate of replacement and your portfolio will plateau.

These are just guestimates because every portfolio is a snowflake. If you are investing at a pace of 2-3 companies a year, you will likely plateau at 10-15 companies, if you invest in 4-6 companies a year, you will plateau in the 15-30 range, and 7-10 companies a year, you will probably plateau in the 30-50 company range.

> Regardless of the **target angel allocation**, those three variables are going to determine how many companies you can do.

Q

If you were giving advice to a new angel investor, what do you think is the minimum number of investments needed to have any real diversification in their angel portfolio?

You might get a lot of nice little wins along the way, but the majority of your returns are going to come from a tiny fraction of your investments. Massive wins are really rare, no matter who you are, and no matter where you are. Given that you are relying on big, rare wins to power the bulk of your returns, it stands to reason that you want to maximize your chance of hitting those. Being good at picking great companies is important, helping your companies succeed is important, and following on in your early breakouts is important. At the end of the day, the most influential factor is having enough mathematical chances to even be in a big winner at all. If you invest in 10 companies you have 5 companies that might be big. If you invest in 20 companies you are fishing out of a pond of 10. And so on. So as far as I am concerned, baseline absolute minimum diversification starts at 10 investments, but this is a case where more is definitely better (again, subject to your ability to manage them as noted above.) Analysts have done Monte Carlo simulations that show that median returns increase substantially with portfolio size. So, while your mileage may vary, it is pretty safe to say that 20 companies is better than 10 and 50 is better than 20.

Q

What is a good pace for making new investments on an annual basis? At that pace, how many investments should an angel expect to have in a mature portfolio?

I think the best thing you can do is to keep the pace of investments relatively high so you can get up the diversification and learning curves quickly, but keep the average first round check size modest so that you have the capital to sustain your pace over the long term, including follow-ons. Follow-on investing is a really big factor in capital use. Getting more money into winners as they start to break out is critical to good returns.

Not all of your companies will merit follow-on investing and the amount of capital required will vary, but a good rule of thumb is to set aside one dollar in follow-on money for every dollar of first round investment. So you want to pick a pace that allows you to keep adding companies, covering your follow-ons and getting into the experienced end of the learning curve where you are presumably going to make better decisions. So when you net it out, to me, if you have the capital, and the time, and the quality deal flow, a good pace of investments is probably around 5-7 deals a year. If you have less time, less capital, and less deal flow, I still think you should be shooting for 3-4.

Q

You spent most of your career in the Enterprise Software industry. Do you make most of your investment in Enterprise Software companies?

No. The industry you know is certainly your comfort zone and your zone of greatest self-sufficiency, but the beauty of angel investing is that, unlike making a career bet where you have to bet it all on one particular job, you can diversify yourself into different industries by collaborating with other investors who have complimentary skill sets. So I definitely invest outside of enterprise software. The closer a company is to that kind of business, the easier it is, and the farther away it is, the harder it is, but my portfolio is well over half outside of enterprise software. One note of caution here is that some industries like life sciences are so radically different due to regulatory issues, IP issues, company development paths, exit dynamics, that if you don't have a background in it, you really need to work closely with expert co-investors for a long time before you can do it on your own. For example, although I have been looking at a lot of life science deals for the last 5 years or so, and I have invested in a few, I feel that I am still years away from being able to do that kind of investing competently on my own. A second note I would make, this time a positive one, is that if you are fascinated in an area and tend to think about it and pay attention to it in your free time, general reading, networking and other activities, you can greatly shorten the time it takes to get up to speed in that area.

Q

How confidently do you invest in companies that are outside your area of expertise?

That's a trick question! Start-ups invent new and innovative ways to fail every day, so I am never objectively confident in any investment I make. You need to have the humility to realize you are going to get burned on a number of them. But that said, many of them fail because of familiar and recognizable issues, and with practice you can spot those issues looming. Also, the quality of the team is a universally important driver in all companies, and some aspects of that team evaluation have common denominators across all industries. So there are some obvious issues you can learn to avoid, some key attributes you can learn to look for, and some personal industry experience you can rely on. As a result, as I have become more experienced, I have grown a bit more confident, or at least a little more trusting of my gut.

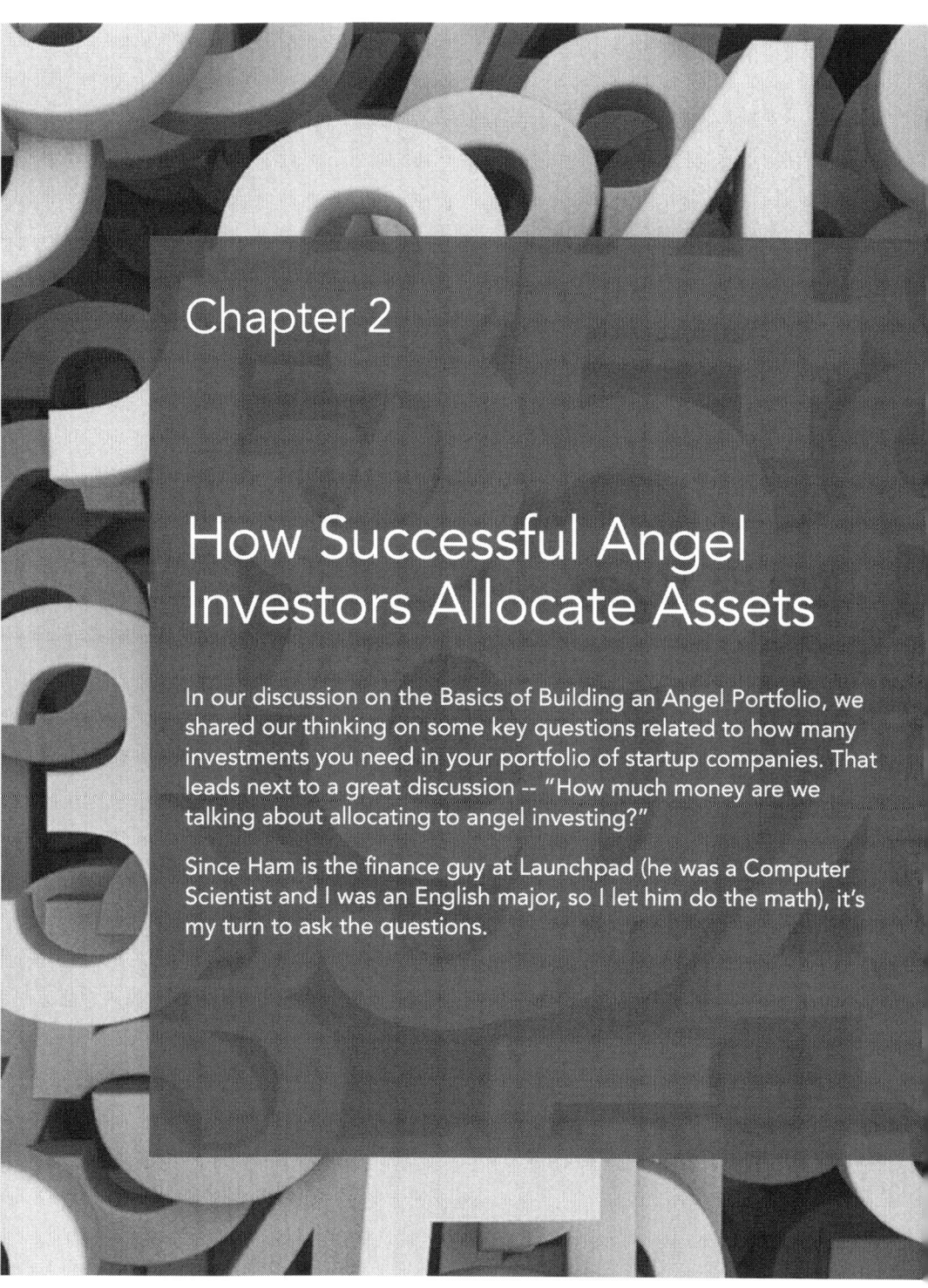

Chapter 2

How Successful Angel Investors Allocate Assets

In our discussion on the Basics of Building an Angel Portfolio, we shared our thinking on some key questions related to how many investments you need in your portfolio of startup companies. That leads next to a great discussion -- "How much money are we talking about allocating to angel investing?"

Since Ham is the finance guy at Launchpad (he was a Computer Scientist and I was an English major, so I let him do the math), it's my turn to ask the questions.

Q

Ham, after 15 years as an active angel investor, how much of your overall investment portfolio is allocated to angel investments? Should it be more? Should it be less?

Even though I began investing many years ago, I began at a measured pace. So it's taken me close to 15 years to grow my angel portfolio to about 15% of my overall investment portfolio. Public companies, REITs, and ETFs make up the majority of my investments. They provide me with a stable source of income and flexibility because they are dividend generating, liquid investments. I can buy and sell them whenever I like. As you know, investing in early stage companies doesn't provide any current income and the investments are not liquid. It's extremely difficult to sell these securities.

The answers to your questions about should it be more or less is a very personal choice. The way I look at it is I have financial responsibilities to my family. Being a more aggressive angel investor would limit our choices as a family in the near term. I'm not willing to make those sacrifices right now. But, a 15% allocation to angel investing means I am deeply involved in this asset class and I am able build a portfolio that is reasonably large at 30+ companies.

Q

You are a pretty active angel, how does 15% compare with other angel investors?

When new angels ask me how much they should invest in this asset class, I typically respond with a range of 5% to 10%. And, I tell them to include any investments they made in venture funds, PE funds, or angel funds in that total allocation.

Based on my experience talking with hundreds of angels over the years, I believe most active angels invest within this range. That said, I also know angels who invest significantly more than this. In almost all of those cases, they are very high net worth individuals and angel investing is their full time job.

> When new angels ask me **how much they should invest** in this asset class, I typically respond with a range of 5% to 10%.

Q

What advice would you give a new angel just starting out? How much capital should they expect to invest on an annual basis if they want to build a diversified portfolio?

Are you ready to do some math?? Here's how I look at it. In the previous chapter, I asked you how many investments an angel should make to build a diversified portfolio. At the low end, you suggest that 10 is the minimum and 20 is better. Furthermore, you suggest that a pace of 3 to 5 new investments per year is a good pace. And finally, you recommend that an angel should reserve a dollar for every dollar invested in the first round.

I agree with your suggestions, so how does that translate into an annual capital commitment? Let's make the following assumptions:

- You invest in 3 new companies per year at $10,000 each
- You invest an additional $10,000 in each company some time within 18 months of making the first investment in that company

So that will work out to $30,000 in your first year and $50,000+ in subsequent years. For someone who invests $25,000 in each new company, the numbers look more like $75,000 in the first year and $125,000+ in subsequent years. Not everyone believes in follow-on investing, so their capital commitments will be lower on an annual basis. Without the follow-on rounds, an angel will cut their capital commitment in half.

As a side note, at Launchpad we highly recommend new angels start out investing at the $10,000 level. It's better to get your feet wet by doing more deals and smaller investments.

We always cringe when a new member of our group writes a $50,000 check for their first investment. We feel they are setting themselves up for an unsustainable investment pace and an unavoidable case of buyer's remorse.

Q

How much capital should they allocate for their entire angel portfolio?

After 4 full years based on the above scenario, you will have a portfolio with approximately 12 companies (don't forget you might have an early failure or acquisition), and you will have invested somewhere in the neighborhood of $200,000 to $250,000. Not coincidentally, I believe this is the minimum amount you should reserve for building an angel investment portfolio. Anything less than that amount and you won't have invested in enough companies. So if you aren't comfortable committing $250,000 to angel investing over a 4 year period, you might not want to start.

Let's examine another scenario. If an angel builds a portfolio closer to your recommended range of 20+ companies where the investment pace is 6 new deals a year, the math works out to something like this: Assuming $25,000 for the initial round and allocating funds for follow-on rounds, an angel will invest over $1,000,000 dollars in a 4 to 5 year time frame. If you keep to the 5% to 10% of your overall investable net worth, such an angel should have an overall investment portfolio of between $10,000,000 and $20,000,000.

Q

What do you do when one of your angel investments returns capital to you?

Since starting out as an angel investor in 2000, I've had quite a few exits. The positive ones range from a 2x return to an 11x return. It's not enough to launch me into the ranks of the Forbes Billionaire List, but it is enough to keep me going as an active angel. My approach to investing is to take any returns I receive and reinvest in new startup companies. I treat my angel portfolio as an evergreen fund, and based on my exits, I am able to grow my portfolio with many more new investments.

> I treat my angel portfolio as **an evergreen fund**, and based on my exits, I am able to grow my portfolio with many more new investments.

Q

What about Crowdfunding platforms... can't I just invest a few thousand dollars using them?

Crowdfunding platforms have features like syndicates that allow you to write smaller checks, and they allow people in areas with less deal flow to gain access to deals they might not otherwise see. But these advantages need to be balanced against two key countervailing issues.

First is the fact that the above advantages relate to the financial capital side of the ledger. In angel investing, the human capital side of the ledger is equally important, if not more important. Some important issues to keep in mind include:

- The financial capital advantages must be weighed against the fact that you are not meeting the teams and making any kind of direct assessment;
- You do not know whether anyone did any real diligence, or if done, who did the diligence;
- You do not know the quality of the deal lead;
- You do not know who, if anyone, is putting in coaching, mentoring, and advising work;
- Your class of investors may not be getting a board seat, or if they are, you do not have any connection to the person taking the seat, nor any ability to asses the value they bring;
- You do not know if the deal lead has any rational plan in terms of

staging capital into the company over the long term; and
- You do not know what company updates or information will filter down to you, making the absolutely critical question of whether to follow on nearly impossible to assess.

Second is the fact that many of these platform systems have the added risk of potential "adverse selection" - the phenomenon whereby the good deals may already be filled before they get to the platform. The issue here is that for a given company, the theoretically lowest cost of capital is a quick local round filled by quality investors from your community who know and trust you and each other. The farther the company has to go from that theoretical ideal, and the more it has to pay in fees, time, and work to access capital, the more difficulty it may be presumed to have had raising the lower-cost capital. There are exceptions to this, but as a general matter, if some companies are going to platforms to "fill out their rounds" doesn't that mean that the converse is also true? That companies who were able to fill their rounds are not on the platform? If so, does that make you the person filling out rounds that are having trouble getting filled? There is a potential risk somewhere in here, and it is compounded by the lack of direct connection to the company as described in the preceding paragraph.

So, while you can use platforms to diversify (especially geographically) and write far smaller checks, it is foolish to think there are any shortcuts in this very labor-intensive asset class - as my partner Christopher likes to point out, angel investing really is not something that can be done properly with a web browser, while sitting at home wearing your slippers.

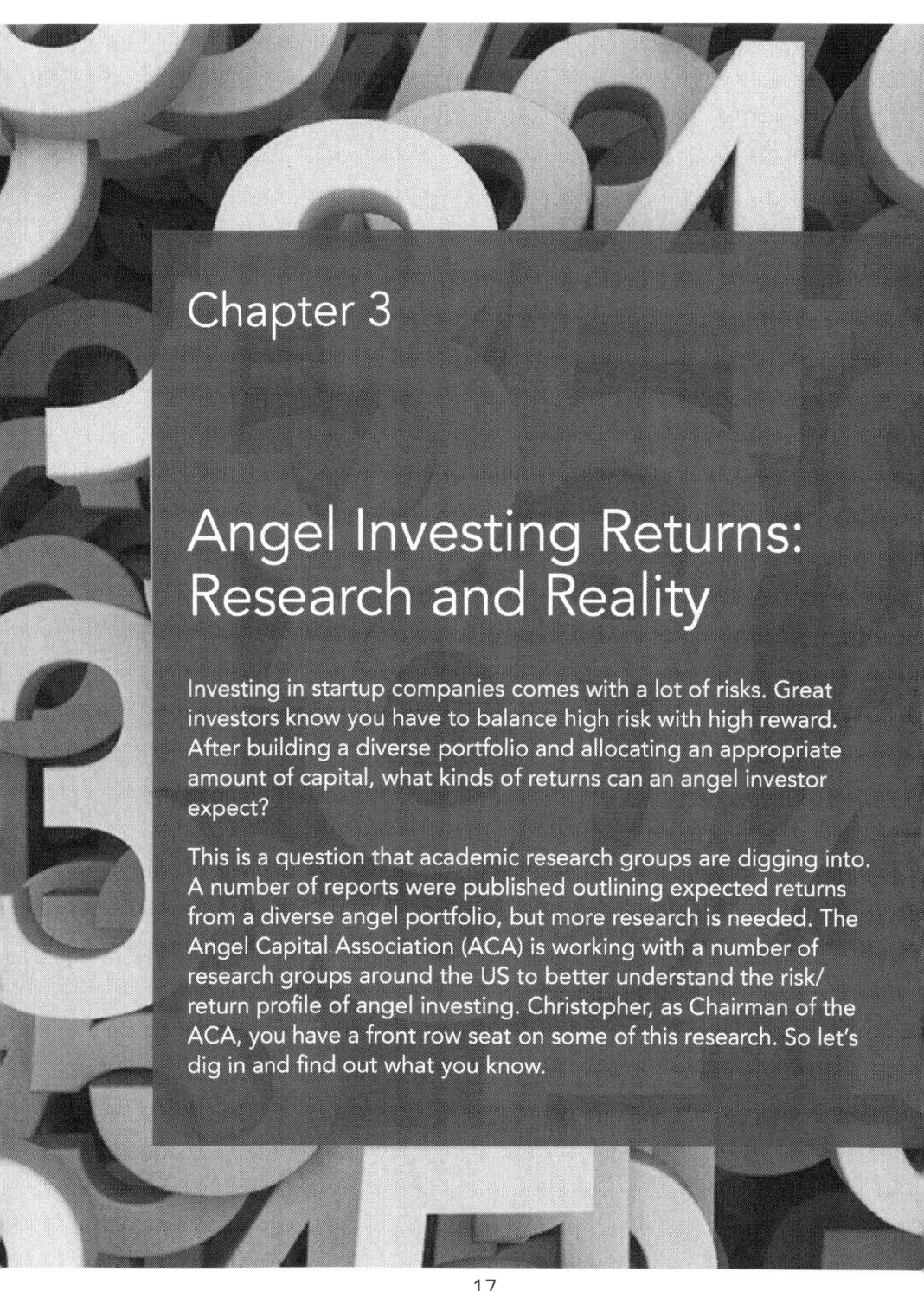

Chapter 3

Angel Investing Returns: Research and Reality

Investing in startup companies comes with a lot of risks. Great investors know you have to balance high risk with high reward. After building a diverse portfolio and allocating an appropriate amount of capital, what kinds of returns can an angel investor expect?

This is a question that academic research groups are digging into. A number of reports were published outlining expected returns from a diverse angel portfolio, but more research is needed. The Angel Capital Association (ACA) is working with a number of research groups around the US to better understand the risk/return profile of angel investing. Christopher, as Chairman of the ACA, you have a front row seat on some of this research. So let's dig in and find out what you know.

Q

Tell us a bit about the research studies that were completed a few years ago. What organizations did the research? How did they go about collecting and analyzing the data?

As a general matter this is an area that is under-studied, and difficult to study, because it is incredibly dispersed, informal and unregulated. That said, there have been a couple attempts at both sizing the angel market and analyzing returns.

On market sizing, Jeffrey Sohl at the Center for Venture Research is probably the most authoritative and transparent, although other studies have come up with fairly similar corroborating results using different methods. CVR's excellent series of studies sizes the angel market at an average of about $22.3B per year over the period 2001-2014, with the size averaging about $23B in the 2001-2007 period, dropping to an average of about $19B per year in the recession years of 2008-2010 and an average of about $24B since then.

In terms of average returns, the largest and most widely-cited study was done in 2007 by Robert Wiltbank and Warren Boeker with funds from the Ewing Marion Kauffman Foundation. That study looked at the returns of 3,097 investments by 538 angels and included data on 1,137 exits and closures. The findings of that study were that the average return was 2.6 times the investment in 3.5 years, or an IRR of 27%. According to an excellent survey of other returns studies done by a group called Right Side Capital Management, the returns findings of most other studies tend to cluster around this IRR, save for one low outlier at 18% and one high outlier at 37%.

Q

In addition to returns data, what are some of the other key findings from these reports?

Aside from returns, the Wiltbank/Boeker study had three very three key findings:

1. Angels who put in more due diligence time (20-40 total person hours per deal) had better returns,

2. Angels who had expertise or access to expertise in their investing areas had better returns, and

3. Angels who interacted with their portfolio companies at least a couple times per month with mentoring, coaching, providing leads and monitoring performance had better returns.

Q

What are some of your personal experiences for the returns you've had in the first 7 years that you have been an active angel investor?

I have invested in 41 companies directly and I am an investor in two low fee/low carry angel funds. The two funds are diversification plays (one vertical and one geographical) and each of them will yield me ownership in about 35-45 additional companies. Neither fund has experienced any positive or negative exits so far. As for my direct investments, it is still relatively early at only 7 years for the oldest companies and far fewer years for lots of them, but I have experienced nine exits so far. Four were positive returns, and five returned less than 100 cents on the dollar.

Aggregated, those nine exits have generated about a 56% return on the total money invested in the nine winners and losers or a 1.56X and an IRR of around 17% (all pre-tax numbers). However, consider that you tend to get your failures faster than your wins, and that you get smarter over time. So in my case, when I look at the money that remains at work in various interesting companies, I have what I believe is a very reasonable basis for excitement about excellent overall potential returns. And of course, I continue to add interesting new companies every year!

Q

What can you tell us about some of the research that the ACA is collaborating on with other organizations?

The Angel Capital Association partners with its sister organization, the Angel Resource Institute, to do a variety of education and research activities. The most notable is a long running data collection effort called the Halo Report which collects investment activity data from the ACA's 13,000+ member angels. There is also an initiative underway to update the performance data in the 2007 Wiltbank/Boeker study. In addition, the ACA is constantly surveying its members on a variety of topics and has recently formed a small fund in collaboration with Rev1 Ventures in Columbus Ohio to honor legendary angel John Huston and to support research on American angels. That study will look at qualitative questions about angels: who they are, what they invest in, and what they care about.

Q

Some angel investors tell me they aren't all that interested in financial returns. They claim they do angel investing for the psychic returns.

Can you explain what they mean by "Psychic Returns"?

The money involved in angel investing is serious, so I have yet to meet a single angel who literally did not care at all about the financial returns, but that said, most angels do cite the rewarding nature of the work as part of the reason they spend so much time and effort in angel investing. Many angels are people who were successful in life through some combination of hard work, skill, and luck, and many of these people want to give back. Few things in life are more rewarding than using your knowledge and experience to help other people succeed. The fun and satisfaction associated with getting involved in a fascinating project and seeing it through to a successful conclusion is what people are referring to when they talk about the psychic returns of angel investing. If that project also has a positive social impact by making the world a better, healthier or more convenient place, or delivers a financial return for the founders and the investors, that turbo-charges the psychic returns.

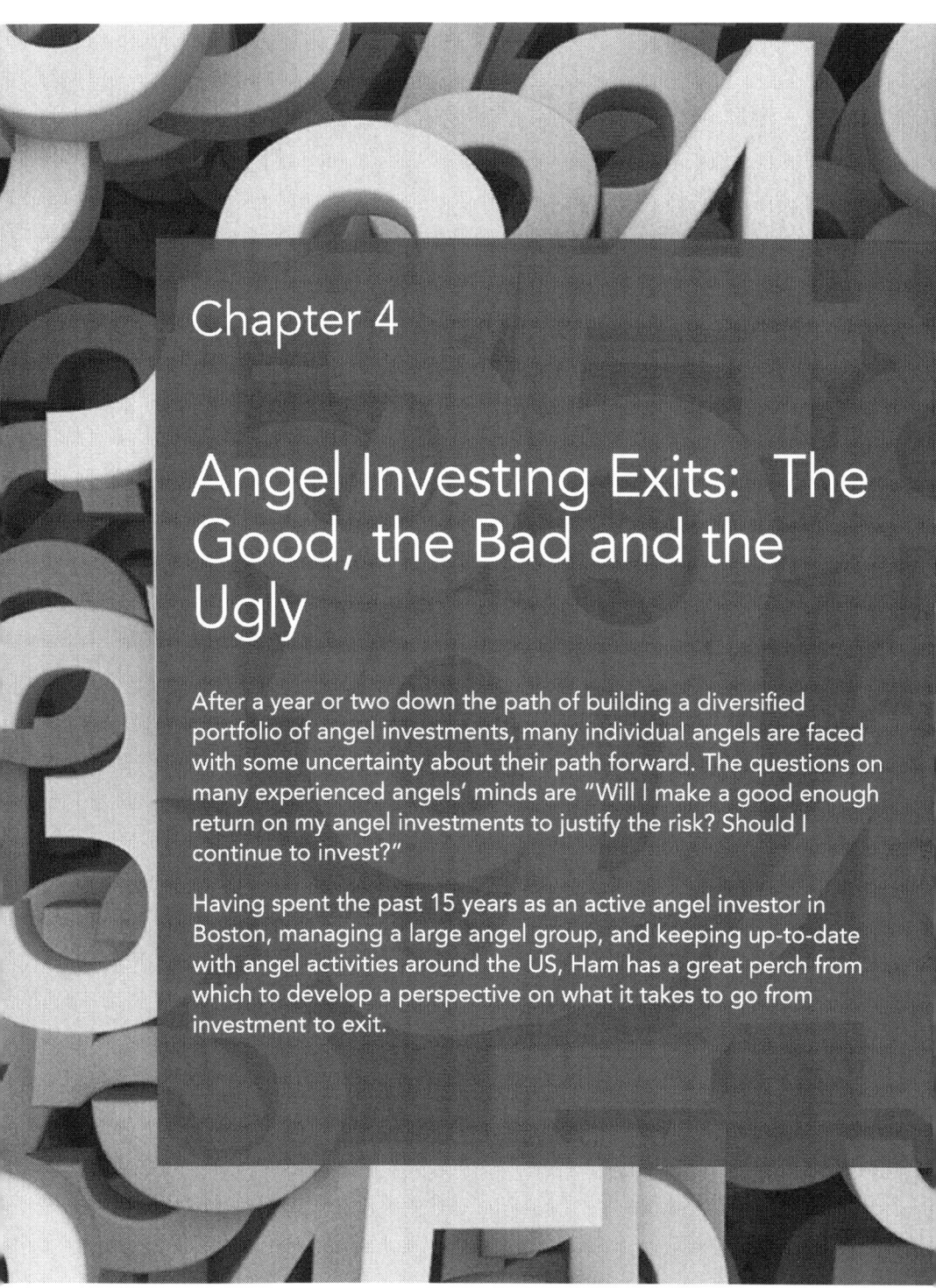

Chapter 4

Angel Investing Exits: The Good, the Bad and the Ugly

After a year or two down the path of building a diversified portfolio of angel investments, many individual angels are faced with some uncertainty about their path forward. The questions on many experienced angels' minds are "Will I make a good enough return on my angel investments to justify the risk? Should I continue to invest?"

Having spent the past 15 years as an active angel investor in Boston, managing a large angel group, and keeping up-to-date with angel activities around the US, Ham has a great perch from which to develop a perspective on what it takes to go from investment to exit.

Q

At Launchpad, we worked on a research project to understand the different kinds of exits we had in our portfolio. Give us a summary on the research methodology and findings?

At the time of our research project in the Fall of 2012, we had 17 exits in our angel group (it's now about 24 exits). About half the exits were positive exits and the other half each returned less than we originally invested. The sample size we examined was large enough to gather some interesting insights. We looked at each company and recorded the following data:

- Time from initial investment to exit
- Total number of rounds of investment
- Types of investors (e.g. Angels, VCs, Corporate Investors, Friends & Family)
- And finally, the amount of capital returned to investors

The chart on the next page provides a visual explanation of what exits look like in the context of startup companies. We think this chart gives a great overview of what angel investors can and should expect within their angel investment portfolio.

So let's walk through this chart in more detail. The arrows that point down represent the different ways companies fail and return less than the capital originally invested. These companies may return some capital, but for you the angel investor, you will see little return.

Fail Fast on Seed Only: If you are doing a good job finding companies, performing due diligence, and sizing the initial rounds to get to key milestones, there should be a limited number of companies in your portfolio that fail quickly. In our portfolio, these companies were usually characterized as early seed deals where a great idea didn't pan out. The company raised a small amount of capital, but the technology didn't work, or customers weren't interested in buying for any one of a whole host of reasons. As seed investors, you decide to stop funding the company and the company can't find any other investors. Although losing all your money in a seed deal doesn't feel great, typically you put a small amount of money into the company at this stage. So your overall loss in time and money tends to be low. Remember, the only thing worse than a mistake, is an expensive mistake. A typical Fast Fail scenario has less than $1M invested in the company, and it took less than 18 months to fail.

Fail After Multiple Angel Rounds: This is probably the most common scenario for failed angel deals. You find a great team with an awesome product. The company makes some early progress, but not enough to raise a large follow-on round of financing. So you and your angel colleagues pony up a bridge round to help the company achieve the milestones that the big investors need to see. One bridge round turns into two or three bridge rounds, with the plausibility of each successive round buttressed by the human tendency to not want to admit you were wrong until you are absolutely forced to. So you chip into the pot to see the next card. Before you know it, you've invested 2x or 3x what you put into the first round, and it's four years after you made your initial investment. And, the company continues to underachieve. At this point, the old investors are ready to bail, and new investors aren't

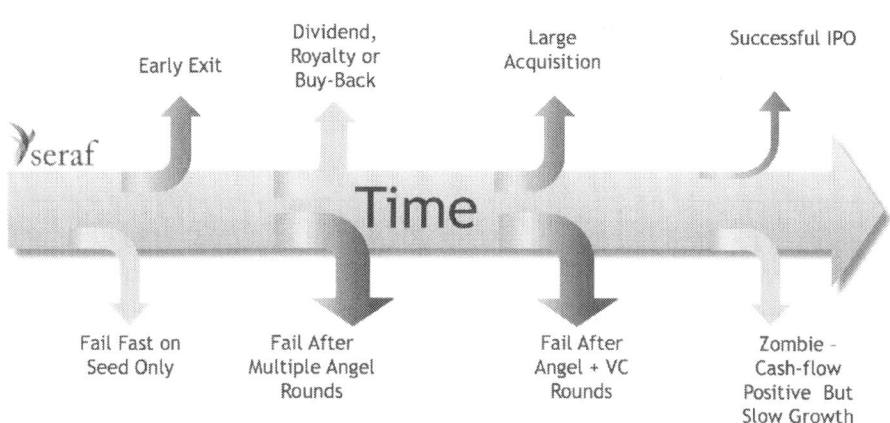

interested. So, if you are lucky, you unload the company at a fire sale price to some other company. In the end, you lost much, if not all, of your investment and you spent 4 years going through this exercise. A typical scenario in this situation has $1M to $3M invested in the company over a 3 to 5 year time frame.

Fail After Angel and VC Rounds: Some of the most promising startups end up in this bucket. The story goes something like this... you invest in the seed round, the company gets some early traction and shows good signs of product/market fit. Times are buoyant, competition for good deals is hot so VCs start to take interest and the company closes a Series A round of financing at a nice step up in valuation. On paper, your seed investment is now worth 3x what you invested. Things are looking good! Unfortunately, the initial success doesn't pan out and growth stalls at the company. But, no one is willing to call it quits, so the VCs force a pivot or maybe some change to management and the company raises additional rounds of financing. Your initial stake in the company keeps getting diluted unless you pony up with additional funds at increasing valuations. In the end, the company gets sold or shut down and your return is zero. A typical scenario in this situation has $10M to $20M invested in the company over a 7 to 10 year time frame.

Zombie - Cash Flow Positive, but Slow Growth - No Liquidity: We've all invested in companies like this. The business grows slowly but surely. Revenues climb into the millions and the company can easily stay around cash flow break-even because it is only making modest investments in growth. However, the growth rate for the business is in the low single digits, the company cannot attract a big slug of capital to force growth, and the company remains below the radar of any potential buyer. This situation is relatively common with angel backed companies and less so with VC backed companies. The main reason for this is that VCs have to distribute the assets of their fund to their investors around the 10 to 13 year mark. Having to distribute stock in a private company is not ideal. So many VCs will force the sale of a zombie-like company. Angels are less motivated to force the sale of a company, so they end up holding their investment for much longer than they ever expected. Many zombies are just life style companies in disguise. The founding team has no motivation to sell because there are no interesting offers, they are drawing a nice salary and aren't working as hard as they did in the early startup days. If you are an investor in a company that fits this description, get together with the other investors and work with the CEO to come up with an exit plan.

> One bridge round turns into two or three bridge rounds, with the plausibility of each successive round buttressed by the human tendency to not want to admit you were wrong.

Q

So we reviewed the not so good exits, but what about the positive exits?

This is the fun and lucrative part of angel investing. What do those exits look like? Let's revisit the chart we showed before, but this time we will examine the upward pointing arrows.

Early Exit: One of the great things about being an angel investor versus being a VC is you don't have to swing for the fences with every at bat. Sometimes a double or a triple is a great exit for you as long as it doesn't take too long to happen. If you double your money in under 2 years, your IRR is around 40%. I'll take that level of return any time! Especially considering that I can immediately turn that money around and put it back into a new investment for the chance of an additional return on the money. Positive early exits usually fall into one of the following categories:

- A new product that complements a fast growing, large company's product line

- A disruptive product that has the potential to damage a larger company's market position
- A new product that fills a newly emerging gap in a big company's product line
- A new product with strategic patents that a buyer cannot risk having fall into a competitor's hands
- A new technology or business model that is so innovative that the opportunity to get the team and the goodwill around the brand is irresistible
- A new product that is clearly constrained by lack of sales and that would be instantly accretive and profitable in the hands of a larger sales force.

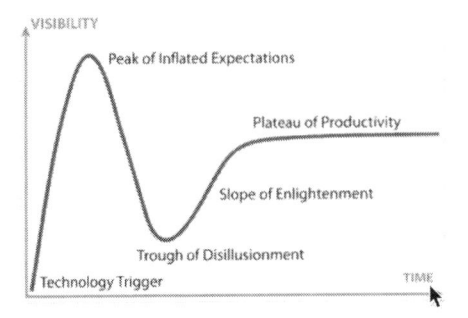

[Gartner Hype Cycle chart: Visibility vs. Time, showing Technology Trigger, Peak of Inflated Expectations, Trough of Disillusionment, Slope of Enlightenment, and Plateau of Productivity]

As we can see from the Gartner Hype Cycle chart, early exits are best timed when a company is at the stage of "Peak of Inflated Expectations". This tends to occur right about the time a company first releases a product, or when they get very positive results from early clinical trials in the case of a Life Sciences company. If you wait much beyond this peak, company value can drop significantly. Selling the dream is often much easier than selling the reality.

Dividend, Royalty or Buy Back: Although these three options represent less than 10% of exits in angel investing, they do happen. In most cases, startup companies burn a lot of cash and don't have the ability to fund a dividend payout. But there are times when a company grows to a stage where additional investment isn't needed or is not going to materially affect the valuation for any of the logical buyers, and the board decides to distribute some of the extra cash as dividends while the company is looking for a buyer. In contrast, royalty payment exits happen when angel investors structure the initial investment so the exit for the investors will be through a royalty payment instead of a buyout upon sale of the business.

The Buy Back scenario has at least two flavors. In one scenario, the company buys back shares from any investor who is interested in selling. These buy backs tend to be at a decent, but limited return to investors, and will often come at a "liquidity discount" relative to fair market value. The second case occurs when a new investor in the company (e.g. a large VC) wants to buy more stock in a company than the company wants to sell. The new investor, with agreement by the board, then reaches out to current investors offering to buy some or all of their shares. This type of exit can be quite lucrative to early investors. We've seen situations where shares were bought at a 5X+ premium after investors held the stock for less than 2 years.

Large Acquisition: By far the most common type of big exit for angel investors is by way of a cash acquisition by a larger company that can use its highly-liquid public shares as currency. This scenario represents a fast way to get cash returned to you without any lockup on selling from an IPO or from an acquisition by another privately held company. In many cases, these acquisitions include a substantial upfront payment and then a smaller (10 - 25%) escrow payment that will pay out in 12 to 18 months. For Life Science companies, it's also common to see milestone payments and royalties, where increasingly larger amounts of capital are returned to investors as the company's product makes it through different stages of clinical trials all the way through to FDA approval and product sales.

Successful IPO: Although IPOs are currently much less common than in recent decades, most investors still see an IPO as the Holy Grail of angel investing. It certainly gives you awesome bragging rights at cocktail parties, and a great return for your portfolio! But IPOs are a rare beast these days, particularly smaller sub-$100M ones. They still happen, but companies are staying private much longer and going out at much higher valuations than ten to twenty years ago. Given current regulations in the US, and the fact that these IPOs offer much less in the way of headline-grabbing first day "pop" than the old days, it's doubtful that the appetite for IPOs on the part of either the public or CEOs will rebound much higher any time soon. When they happen they can be awesome returns, but just be aware that you won't be able to sell your stock during the approximate 6 month lock-up period after the company first goes public.

Q

It has been said that you find out about your mistakes pretty quickly. What situations result in an exit occurring within the first 1 to 3 years?

As we discussed earlier in this chapter, in our portfolio, these companies were usually characterized as early seed deals where a great idea didn't pan out. The company raised a small amount of capital, but the technology didn't work, or customers weren't interested in buying for any one of a whole host of reasons. As seed investors, you decide to stop funding the company and the company can't find any other investors. Although losing all your money in a seed deal doesn't feel great, typically you put a small amount of money into the company at this stage. So your overall loss in time and money tends to be low. Remember, the only thing worse than a mistake, is an expensive mistake.

In some cases you don't lose all your capital. If the founding team is solid, it's not unusual for a larger company to acquire the failed company for their talented team and pay a modest amount to the early investors. Also, be aware of the tax benefits from IRS tax code section 1244 that might allow you to write off your loss versus your earned income instead of at the lower rate of capital gains.

Q

In your personal portfolio and the Launchpad portfolio, describe some of the successful exits? How long did they take? When is it OK to be patient?

I was an early investor in a company called SmartPak. SmartPak built the number one brand in the Equine market over a decade-long time period. The company achieved strong, steady growth and was very capital efficient along the way. Management understood the importance of building a strong brand, and they did an incredible job of running a lean, efficient business. From initial investment to exit was about 12 years, but the return multiple was 11x.

Launchpad's successes span everything from a quick 1 year exit, to the typical 4 to 7 year exits, and finally 10+ year exits. As you would expect, the quick exits are predominantly 1.5x to 3x level of returns. The 4 to 7 year exits are clustered in a 3x to 8x level of return.

For the 10+ year type of exit, I believe it's okay to be patient as long as the company hasn't raised a lot of capital. For companies that are capital efficient, there isn't a significant overhang from the preference stack (i.e. preferred stock liquidation preferences and dividends). As the clock ticks, dividends can really add up, especially when a company raises $10M or more over time. A large preference stack will cut severely into returns for early investors. At Launchpad, we have one long term investment that raised around $1M in angel money at a low valuation. Based on their current financial metrics, the company should be able to exit with greater than a 10x multiple for the investors.

> As the clock ticks, **dividends can really add up**, especially when a company raises $10M or more over time.

Q

There are lots of stories in the press about the big wins such as Facebook and Google. How common are those exits? Are those kinds of exits limited to consumer internet, or do they happen in other industries?

Returns like 1500x for early eBay investors are an incredibly rare thing, but still fuel the dreams and provide the justifications for many investments, particularly in consumer web and consumer mobile. But these gold rush type returns are super rare and really only associated with massive disruptions like quickly going from no broadband to ubiquitous broadband or slow expensive wireless to fast cheap wireless.

Success in consumer markets easily overshadows success in other industries. However, there are other areas where angel investors should consider. For example, enterprise software companies such as Salesforce.com and Workday have market caps well in excess of $10B. In healthcare, there are a number of successful companies such as Athenahealth, Gilead and Celgene. In some cases, the companies are capital efficient (e.g. Athenahealth), but in others (e.g. Gilead) they are not. So early investors in the life sciences need to be aware of the enormous capital required to turn out a successful company.

Q

If you built a portfolio of 10 companies, what should you expect?

Assuming you are an angel investor who puts time and effort into building your 10 company portfolio by performing due diligence and adding human capital to support your investments, you should have the following expectations

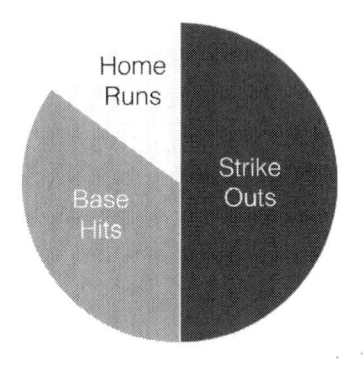

A rough estimate for your portfolio will include 5 failed companies, 4 base hits and 1 home run. Let's break this down a bit further and understand what this will mean for your returns. With the 5 failures, you can expect little if any capital returned. You will have some tax benefits on the losses, but they will add up to around 20-30% of your original investment.

Base hits describe exits anywhere from 1x to 10x of your original investment. As we discussed in a previous question, quick exits will result in a 1.5x to 3x return of capital and the other exits should cluster in the 3x to 8x range.

Your portfolio's one home run should be somewhere greater than a 10x return. Assuming you allocated the same amount of capital to all 10 companies, this company will return all the capital that you invested in the original 10 companies. Think of this exit as 'returning your fund'. But, how you do overall is now driven by how your base hits do. A couple of 5x returns and a couple of 3x returns will help you generate overall fund returns of at least 2.5x your original capital.

Chapter 5

Look Before You Leap: The Importance of Due Diligence in Angel Investing

There are as many different approaches to angel investing as there are investors. Some investors will tell you they invest based on their gut. After a 30 minute meeting with the entrepreneur, they are either in or out. They like to invest in people and that initial meeting guides their decision-making process. Other investors like to dig deep. They will spend significant effort digging into every aspect of a company from team, to market, to competition, to intellectual property and so on. And, there is every variation in between these extremes. For the sake of brevity we will leave out discussing the approach of investing in whatever your buddy is investing in!

Before Christopher joined the world of angel investing, he spent much of his career acquiring smaller companies for the NASDAQ-listed enterprise software company where he was the CFO. He knows what real due diligence is first hand. At Launchpad, he adapts those skills in a way that fits for the type of early stage investing that we do. That said, Christopher will admit that he doesn't always follow his own rules.

Q

Give us three reasons why it's important to do some diligence before you invest in a startup company?

For some reason, in life it seems like it is always faster to imagine the obvious ways something might work than it is to grasp the sometimes subtle and complex ways things could go wrong. Perhaps people are optimists, or perhaps it is the tendency to want to believe an earnestly and passionately-told story from an entrepreneur who is betting their livelihood on it. But whatever the reason, more time spent on due diligence always yields a more balanced and nuanced view. Additional time allows you to get the perspective of different experts, spend time with the team, educate yourself on the market, understand the psyche of the target customer. If you do not take the time to put in a little work, you are just making a blind bet during that overly optimistic honeymoon phase, and you are giving up the chance to consider very easily-discovered issues and to ponder whether it is realistic to expect a team to work around them.

> More **time spent on due diligence** always yields a more balanced and nuanced view.

Q

What areas do you focus on when you are looking at a company? Is there one area that is most important to you?

Team is by far the biggest focal point of my inquiry. Other factors are important, but none has the make-or-break importance of questions around team quality. The issue comes down to a simple realization that an "A team" with a "B plan" will outperform a B team with an A plan every time. Rising market "tides" do help all boats, but not enough to save boats with holes in them or boats with no captain. How do A teams do it? An A team is reading the market all the time. They can tell that it's not coming together. They pivot before they've gotten themselves into such a capitalization hole that there's no way the company can ever perform for investors. A good CEO will pivot, but a great CEO will pivot in a capital-efficient way. She will recognize that the data and the progress are just not there and start to move early and decisively before the company has raised and spent so much money that the cap table is just irretrievably screwed up. That takes vision, courage, humility, communication skills, analytical skills, listening skills, business management savvy, leadership skills, tenacity in the face of disappointment, and grit and determination. Plus maybe a sense of humor and some healthy perspective. These are the things you are looking for. Team chemistry and dynamics are also key - a group of high functioning individuals is different from a high-functioning team.

Secondarily, I focus on market size and segmentation with a particular attention to the number of potential customers for whom the company's solution is a top pain point and a top buying priority. Too many diligence efforts stop at "yup, I am satisfied that there are lots of people out there who would buy this." The question is, where does it lie in their priority list? Are there enough of them who view it as a "need to have" rather than a "nice to have" that reasonable market share represents a big market?

Beyond that, there are a host of other issues you need to consider like the company's defensive and offensive IP situation, the business' inherent margins and long-term defensibility, exit scenarios, capital intensity, deal terms and investor dynamics.

As you can see, there are plenty of things to ponder once you start to create the space to think things through beyond the "yeah, I see how that could work" stage.

Q

How do you go about figuring out the key areas to perform diligence when the companies you look at are in different industries and different stages of development?

Team is always a constant, but on the market analysis side, different industries require different ways of getting into the head of the customer in the target segment. It is not a question of whether you will look at those things, but rather a question of how. For example, some types of opportunities really require grey-haired experience and connections on the founding team in order to understand the problem and break into the market. But in other really disruptive opportunities, such "knowledge" will only serve to limit the team to an "it cannot be done this way" mentality.

> You are always going to need to adjust your approach to make sure you are **giving thought to the key risk factors** and not wasting time on less important issues.

Beyond team and market, some opportunities present very specialized issues. For example, life sciences companies always involve very critical regulatory and reimbursement questions as well as peculiar go-to-market paths and different exit timing and dynamics. Ed Tech companies have very special types of buyers and product adoption patterns. Some technically-innovative companies may present extremely complex technical or scientific questions that are going to require close study by someone with expertise. So beyond a basic set of common-denominator themes, you are always going to need to adjust your approach to make sure you are giving thought to the key risk factors and not wasting time on less important issues.

Q

Can you describe an issue you missed during the diligence process that ended up coming back to bite you when the investment failed a few years down the road?

The most painful issues I missed have clustered around two core areas:

1. Confusing likability or prior accomplishments on the part of an entrepreneur with the competence needed to pull off the current task. I've lost money with entrepreneurs who are great guys or great gals and had accomplished good things in their prior career endeavors, but were completely over their heads and unable to adapt when driving the new opportunity. As a result, I try to think hard about what skills the coming opportunity will require, and make sure the entrepreneur has, or is willing and able to get, those particular skills.

2. Confusing early adopter excitement with true market pull. It has been said that "anybody can get the first 10% of a market" and Geoffrey Moore's *Crossing the Chasm* stands for that proposition. The key to growing a company is finding a big enough market of willing buyers who can be accessed in an affordable way (relative to their lifetime value). The product may be good, and there may be lots of people who might buy it, but unfortunately a company's true market is limited to those customers for whom that purchase is a top pain point and a top buying priority. Often a marginal improvement on a marginal cost is not enough to drive buying behavior in all but the earliest of adopters. So the key is to recognize when you are looking at what is sometimes called false traction and doing some further digging. There is no substitute for talking to real customers and prospects before doing the deal in these situations.

Q

Fess up... I know you invested in companies without doing any significant due diligence. Why did you invest in those companies?

Naturally I prefer to do an appropriate amount of diligence before digging in, and more often than not pass on a round where proper due diligence is not an option. Sometimes it is not possible or feasible and I decide the potential upside of the opportunity is worth the added risk. Situations where diligence is not possible might include attractive rounds that are nearly full and closing imminently or situations where the market does not yet exist or the product category does not yet exist and your diligence conversations would be entirely hypothetical. You can do that work, but it can sometimes be an exercise in confirmation bias - wishful thinking and hearing what you want to hear.

In situations where you are not going to be able to do an appropriate amount of diligence, you can:

- Rely on your own experience
- Look to make sure there are other high quality investors in the round
- Look extra hard at the quality of the team and the personal opportunity cost they are incurring by going after it, and
- You can manage your initial check size and plan to follow on more heavily once there is a bit more data and track record.

It is not a perfect or a desired way to go about things, but sometimes you have to make compromises if you want to build a diversified portfolio with a variety of interesting opportunities.

Chapter 6

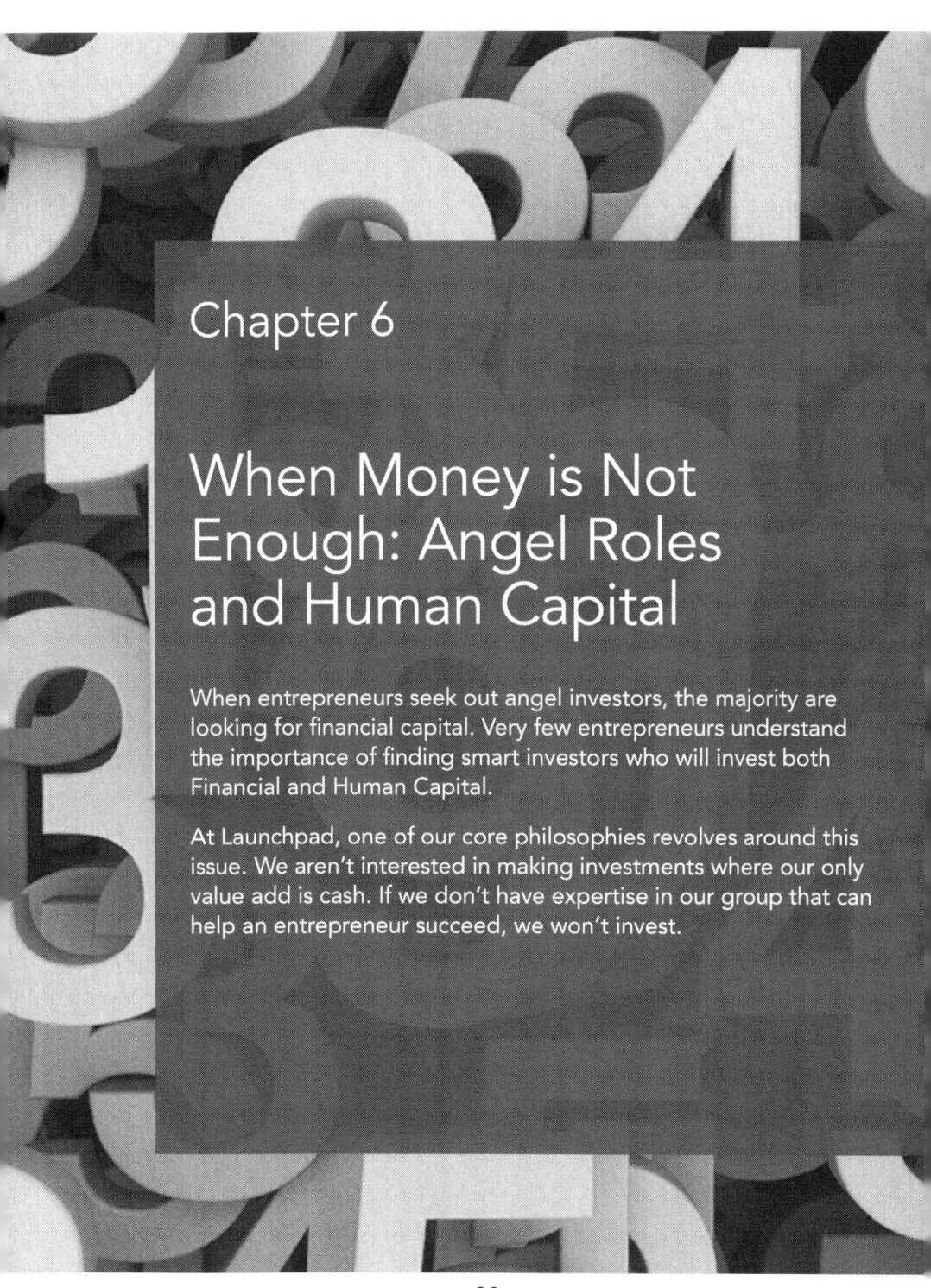

When Money is Not Enough: Angel Roles and Human Capital

When entrepreneurs seek out angel investors, the majority are looking for financial capital. Very few entrepreneurs understand the importance of finding smart investors who will invest both Financial and Human Capital.

At Launchpad, one of our core philosophies revolves around this issue. We aren't interested in making investments where our only value add is cash. If we don't have expertise in our group that can help an entrepreneur succeed, we won't invest.

Ham practices what he preaches. He works closely with many of the companies he invests in, whether as a board member, board observer or just to help out. Having sat on many startup boards since 2002, he understands the kind of Human Capital that angels can provide. And, he witnessed when angels do more harm than good.

Q

What roles do you think angel investors can perform for a startup company?

I like to classify the roles that angel investors take on with a startup in the following three categories. The list starts with the most casual of roles (the mentor) and ends with the most committed of roles (the corporate board member or director).

- Mentor
- Advisory Board Member
- Corporate Board Member

Q

If you could give an entrepreneur advice on working with angels, what would it be?

Communicate, communicate, communicate! Entrepreneurs need to understand that a good angel investor is more than just a walking/talking wallet to keep her company well-funded. If you select your angel investors wisely, you can augment their financial capital with their human capital. So, how do you get the most out of your angel investors' human capital? You communicate with them on a regular basis. We advise CEOs to send out quarterly reports to all investors (and love it when they do monthly). The focus of the report is a business and financial update, but it's important to ask something of the investors. For example, if you are looking to hire a new VP Marketing, do they have any candidates. Or, if you are trying to make inroads into a large company, do they have connections to that company. Even something as simple as requesting that they share a recent piece of content on social media - the key is to keep them engaged.

Q

What are some things angels should be careful never to do?

First of all, angels need to be careful about wasting the time of an entrepreneur. Time is a precious resource for startups, and if you are draining this resource, you are doing more harm than good. Second, entrepreneurs starting their first company have a limited understanding of raising capital for their business. Just because you've made 20 investments doesn't mean you should take advantage of a naive entrepreneur!

Q

Talk a bit more about board seats. What kind of commitment is a board seat for the angel investor?

As a director, you are making a significant human capital commitment to the company. Although you aren't an employee of the company, you are expected to commit your time and expertise to the company. My general expectation for a board seat is that I am committing around 100 hours per year to the company. I break that down as follows:

- 6 to 12 Board meetings/year with 1 hour of prep and 3 hours of meeting time (24 to 72 hours)
- Weekly or bi-weekly phone call with the CEO at 30 minutes per call (13 to 26 hours)
- 10+ activities for other meetings, candidate interviews, fundraising calls, etc. at 1 hour per event (10+ hours)

Board meetings are an obvious commitment for all board members. Good board members read all the board materials in advance and come prepared for the meeting. Between board meetings, I like to stay informed, and so I will arrange for a weekly 30 minute phone call with the CEO. It's scheduled for the same time every week, and gives the CEO an opportunity to ask for my help on tough issues in real time instead of waiting for the next board meeting. And finally, unscheduled events happen with startups. Such events include a job interview for a senior member of management, a compensation committee meeting, or a discussion with a new potential investor.

So that covers the human capital commitment. But what about the financial capital commitment? Since you are an angel investor in the company, you have already invested some of your money. As time goes by, the company will need to raise additional funds. In many cases, board members are the first to commit to new rounds of financing. So keep that in mind as you stage capital for your investment in the company.

> My general expectation for a board seat is that I am **committing around 100 hours per year** to the company.

Q

As a board member, what topics do you focus on when you are speaking with the CEO?

On my weekly phone updates with the CEO, I like to keep it really simple. I start by asking for a quick status update on the business, but I don't dig into the nitty-gritty of the company's daily operations. I spend most of my time discussing the following three topics:

- Team
- Finances
- Strategy

When talking about the "Team", I want to make sure the CEO is spending a significant percentage of her time hiring the right people ("A" players), building a strong company culture, and keeping the organization focused. In our weekly conversations, I am always listening for bottlenecks that might indicate it's time to bring on a new team member. Sometimes it's as simple as hiring an assistant to offload some of the non-critical tasks on the CEO's overburdened desk. Other times it's when the company reaches an inflection point where it's important to bring on board a full-time CFO to make sure the company is receiving the right metrics to help operate and grow the business. The conversation about Team is the most frequent topic on my weekly CEO call. I can't remember the last time I didn't discuss it in one form or another.

With "Finances", the key topic revolves around not running out of money. Startups burn through cash quickly. The biggest mistake a board and CEO make is to not be prepared for replenishing the bank account in time. As a director, you need to make sure the CEO recognizes when the company will be out of cash and then work with the CEO to ensure it doesn't happen. Conversations around Finances are episodic. They are held frequently during periods of fund raising, and then they go away for a quarter or two when the company's bank account has sufficient cash to last out the year.

The final topic, "Strategy", is a bit more nuanced. In my case, I think of strategy along the lines of the company's "North Star". For me, a company's North Star is the beacon by which it navigates. Once you find your North Star, you stick with it and make sure the entire company understands where you are going. I want to make sure the CEO is communicating on a regular basis with the ENTIRE company to keep everyone on course. As a director, you can help the CEO by acting as a sounding board in defining and refining the company strategy. Remember it's not your job to create the strategy and make the CEO follow it. Conversations on Strategy occur on a fairly regular basis.

Chapter 7

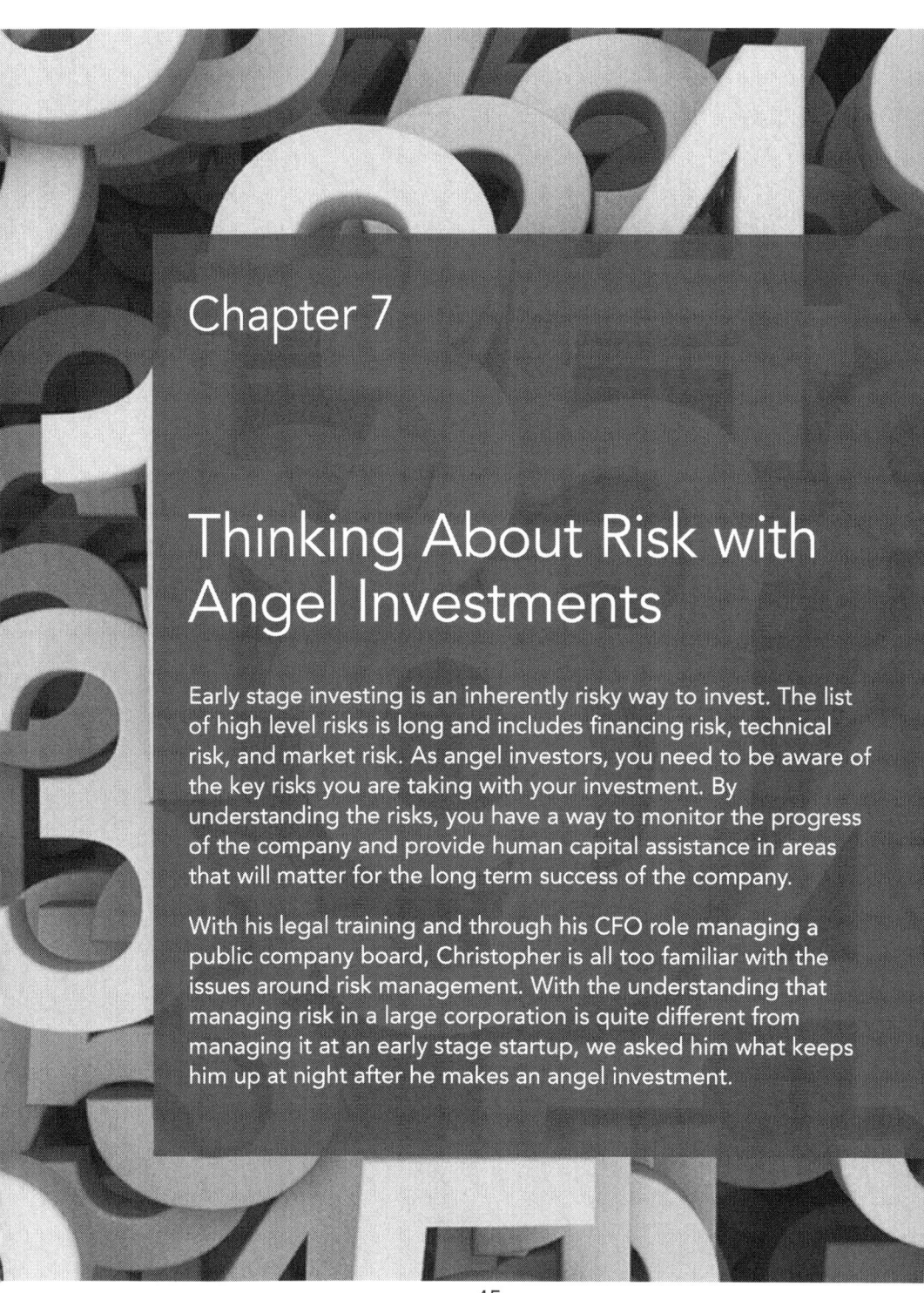

Thinking About Risk with Angel Investments

Early stage investing is an inherently risky way to invest. The list of high level risks is long and includes financing risk, technical risk, and market risk. As angel investors, you need to be aware of the key risks you are taking with your investment. By understanding the risks, you have a way to monitor the progress of the company and provide human capital assistance in areas that will matter for the long term success of the company.

With his legal training and through his CFO role managing a public company board, Christopher is all too familiar with the issues around risk management. With the understanding that managing risk in a large corporation is quite different from managing it at an early stage startup, we asked him what keeps him up at night after he makes an angel investment.

Q

Will you give us a quick summary of the key risk areas that you focus on with startups?

This is not an easy question to answer because every startup situation is a little different, and there are so many nested layers of risk with any start-up. For example, you might wonder "is there an opportunity here?" or you might wonder "is this team good enough to go get it?" or you might wonder "is this company being smart about how it is writing contracts with customers?" or "does this company have complete and up to date personnel records and financial controls?"

Obviously, you cannot evaluate every risk at once, nor would you want to. The key is to focus on the major risks first and leave the secondary and tertiary risks to the side to be addressed at the right time. For example, when you are doing diligence, there is not a lot of point in worrying about the historical board minutes of a company that does not yet have product/market fit.

So as a general matter I try to establish comfort on the big things like whether this is a great team, whether there is a likely big market here and whether there is a smart, defensible and differentiated product. I try to document the key assumptions necessary (what, at Launchpad, we refer to as WNTBB or "what needs to be believed" in order to invest) to get an overall sanity assessment.

Then, once I have a general comfort level on that stuff, I try to get a handle on details around the go-to-market approach, marketing methods, and defensibility of the solution. Only then will I spend time on the financial model to make sure it makes sense. Ultimately, I try to think through the exit options: who are the likely buyers, what aspects of the business will they want, what will they be prepared to pay, and what milestones are going to need to be achieved in order to get bought.

Q

Are there any areas of risk that concern you to a level that you might decide to pass on an investment in a company?

Regulatory risk is obviously a biggie. If the company's legal right to execute its business plan is in doubt for regulatory reasons (for example, FDA approval is required), or the proposed plan is potentially illegal (for example the SEC might decide it is a regulated activity) or it is very dangerous (for example a product associated with ultra hazardous activities or extreme sports that could give rise to huge product liability issues) or the business model is just yucky or misleading (as with certain spammy or privacy invading activities, or certain business models preying on young consumers) then I am probably not going to be interested. One of the nice things about angel investing is that you get to pick whom you do business with and what you get involved in.

Q

What approach do you take when you advise a CEO on how to manage risk?

To be brave and recognize that they are paid the big bucks to take measured risks, that they have to take risks to be successful, and so they cannot obsess about eliminating all risk. After all, if you don't fall down, you are not skiing hard enough. But I also advise them to focus on the really big existential risks and delegate the smaller ones to capable team members. Too many CEOs hold on too tight, to too many silly things, for too long and don't leverage a strong team well enough.

Once the company starts to grow, the risk-taking attitudes will mature and the situation will require a little more conservative and thoughtful approach - in the beginning when the business is nothing and it has no assets, risking it all on a hunch doesn't mean much because the "all" isn't yet a valuable going concern. Once it has a big revenue stream and assets and is responsible for the livelihood of many people, it can be harder to "bet the company". It is still going to be necessary to take big risks, to innovate, to pivot, but it is generally going to take more strategy, planning and thought.

> After all, **if you don't fall down**, you are not skiing hard enough.

Q

As a board member or advisor, what do you do to help the CEO manage risk?

Ask lots of questions starting with "Have you thought about..." or "Have you considered what you'd do if...." or "What are your thoughts on...." Since I am unburdened by the day to day distractions of running the business, it is easier for me to step back and look a little farther down the road. Together we can spot issues a bit earlier and plan for them so that we can take advantage of them rather than just reacting to them in permanent crisis mode.

Q

As a board member or advisor, how do you work with the CEO to monitor and track the progress on risk mitigation?

By helping them develop a good dashboard of all the key performance indicators and monitoring it regularly. If you have the right measures on your dashboard, and you keep your measurement set up to date as the business evolves, it is just a matter of looking at the numbers that are out of whack relative to the initial assumptions and asking "why?" and "what are we missing here?"

Chapter 8

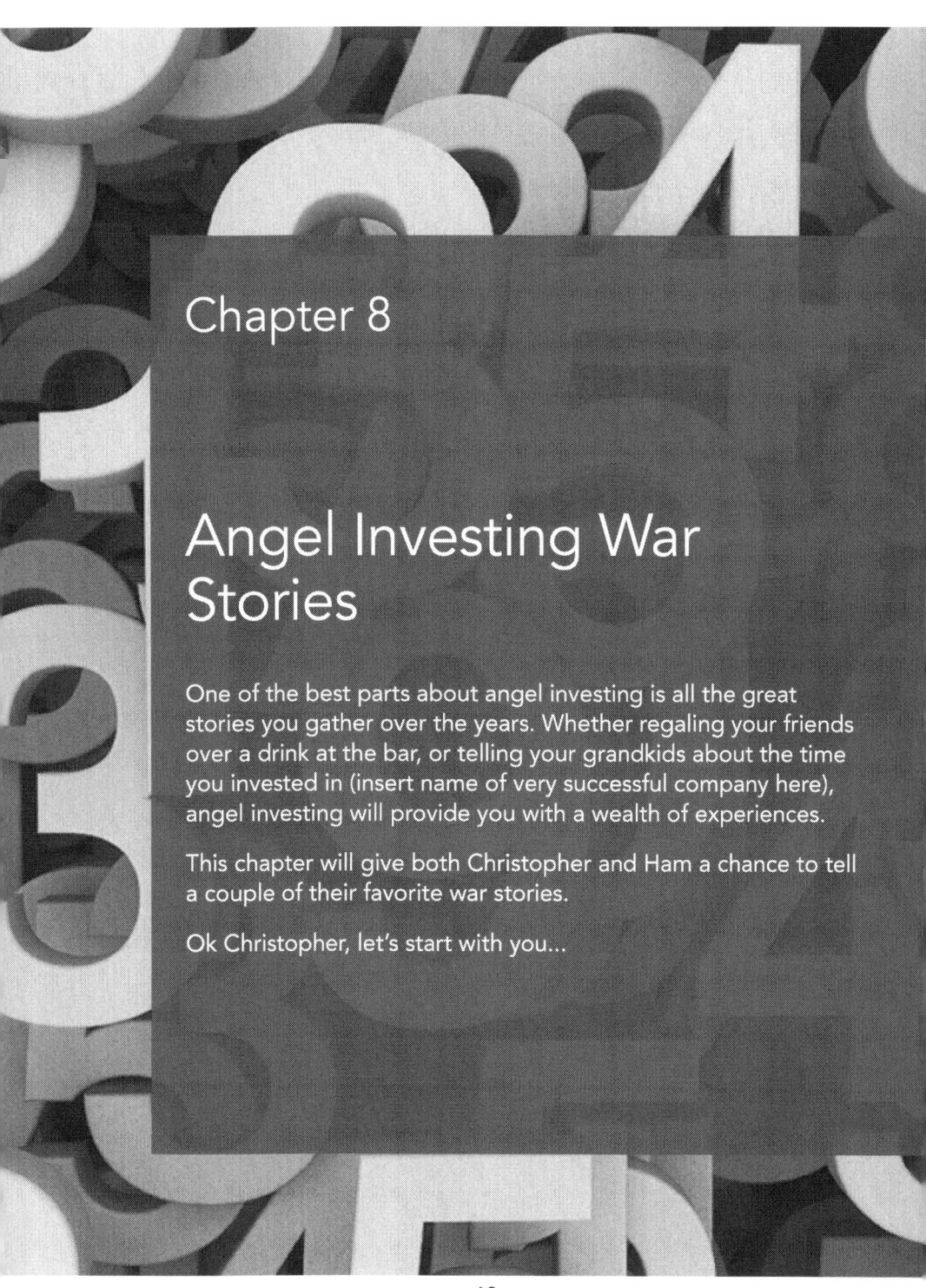

Angel Investing War Stories

One of the best parts about angel investing is all the great stories you gather over the years. Whether regaling your friends over a drink at the bar, or telling your grandkids about the time you invested in (insert name of very successful company here), angel investing will provide you with a wealth of experiences.

This chapter will give both Christopher and Ham a chance to tell a couple of their favorite war stories.

Ok Christopher, let's start with you...

Q

Give us an example of an investment you wouldn't make today, but you did make years ago. How did it turn out? What lessons did you learn?

A few times I have bet on good people I liked, but my motivations were too personal. Liking the person is not enough - you need the rest of the package. In one case I got out alive with a 2X, but the deal terms were awful and the returns should have been much better. In another case the money is probably safe, but the business will never exit, and I will never get liquidity. In the rest of the cases, the businesses were total or near total failures. I've learned the hard way that you need to look for the whole package - check all the boxes - even then you will still be wrong half the time, but if you don't, it is an utter crapshoot.

> I've seen a couple of situations where the **original hypothesis was not working out at all**, and hope was waning, but then a new technology came along and really saved the day.

Q

We've all invested in a sure thing that had many ups and downs. Can you tell us about one of your roller coaster rides?

I've seen a couple situations where the original hypothesis was not working out at all, and hope was waning, but then a new technology came along and really saved the day (interestingly, in both cases it was the iPad and associated use cases that enabled the businesses to come back to life and thrive.) You really feel like you have dodged a bullet when that happens. I guess it is better to be lucky than good! I've also invested in many rounds with one company that launched with a good idea, but it turned out to be horrible timing because it was a luxury/nice-to-have product, and a recession struck right after they launched, so they hit a wall. So they pivoted and next they recycled some of the core skills and went after a totally different market with a totally different product. That market turned out to be really hard to sell to, and growth was elusive, so they had to pivot again. After many rounds of tinkering, they began to dial in on a big pain point for a third, unrelated, customer set. Fast forward to today and they are growing like crazy, have a high valuation, some big investors and very bright prospects. But it was a pretty gut-wrenching 3 years for everyone involved. What ultimately saved them was a very broad and strong investor base who could support the company by passing the hat and everyone chipping in a little, and strong CEO who communicated well to that group.

Now Ham, it's your turn...

Q

Give us an example of an investment you wouldn't make today, but you did make years ago. How did it turn out? What lessons did you learn?

Back in 2003, just after the dotcom bubble burst, it was a difficult time to raise capital for almost any kind of tech startup. One of the few new investments I made that year was in a chip company focused on the consumer electronics industry. The original plan was to develop some core technology, build a great IP portfolio and sell the business. We expected we could accomplish this with a reasonable amount of capital raised primarily from angel investors and maybe a small VC.

Unfortunately, that's not what happened. The new plan required raising a lot of capital from a big VC and building a fabless chip company with both US and overseas operations. To make a long story short, the company was shut down after spending a lot of investor capital. The VC firm wasn't willing to keep funding the business and angel investors don't have the capital reserves to support what was now a capital intensive business.

There were many lessons learned from this investment. The investment was made in the early days of my angel investing career, so I didn't understand what it meant to bring in a large VC firm that had different priorities over the angel investors. So my key takeaway from this failed investment was to make sure all the investors and the management team are in alignment with the business model and the financing strategy. Without alignment, small investors are in a precarious position.

Part Two

Angel 201
The Four Critical Skills Every Angel Investor Should Master

Angel investing started to break into the mainstream in popular American culture in the early 2000s. It started with stories of individuals striking it rich from investments in companies like eBay, Yahoo, PayPal and Google. Silicon Valley garnered most of the headlines, but angel investors increased their activity in other technology centers such as Boston and Seattle and eventually San Diego, Austin and New York. Then, the media began writing about celebrities and athletes making angel investments. Ashton Kutcher, Bono, Kanye West, Justin Timberlake and many others placed their celebrity endorsement on dozens of startups hoping to add to their fortunes. A few of these investments turned out well, but most ended up as write-offs.

Today, one of the most watched shows on TV is *Shark Tank*, which is based on a popular worldwide TV series called *Dragons' Den*. More than 8 million viewers tune into *Shark Tank* every week to watch a reality TV show where entrepreneurs present to a panel of investors, called Sharks. You know things are getting a bit overheated when popular culture embraces an esoteric activity like investing in startup companies! Has angel investing jumped the proverbial shark?? (pun intended!)

All this press and publicity for angel investing makes it sound like anyone can be successful picking companies and throwing a few thousand dollars at the entrepreneur with expectations of riches to follow. Experienced angel investors know this gross misperception will lead to a lot of disappointment. Angel investing isn't easy. Sure, you might get lucky once or twice, but that's no different than betting on a roulette wheel.

Christopher and I take angel investing seriously. It's our full time job and we work hard at it. As an important part of running our angel group, Launchpad Venture Group, we expend significant effort and time training our members on key concepts to help make them better angel investors. Our introductory course, aptly called Angel 101, focuses on topics such as the the basics of building an angel portfolio, expectations on time to exit, expectations on financial return, the importance of due diligence, the risks in early stage companies, and the importance of investing both financial and human capital.

Our next section, Angel 201, digs into 4 critical skills that we believe every angel investor needs to develop. These skills take time and many experiences to establish. The more entrepreneurs you talk to, the smarter you will become. The more investments you make, the better you will get at understanding early stage company financing issues. Over a series of chapters, we will break these four critical skills down:

1. How to evaluate a startup's management team (and the CEO in particular)
2. How to evaluate products and market opportunities
3. How to stage financial capital and make sure a company is properly financed
4. How to plan, optimize and manage an angel portfolio in a tax efficient and organized manner

With mastery of these skills, an angel investor has the tools needed to build a substantial portfolio based on solid investment decisions, not a collection of lottery tickets.

Chapter 9

Rule #1 About Angel Investing: It's All About the Team

Great ideas are a dime a dozen. Living in the Boston/Cambridge area, we are surrounded by some of the most innovative researchers in the world working at institutions like MIT and Harvard. I'm pretty confident when I say, in Boston, hardly a day goes by when some graduate student or professor doesn't invent a new product, discover a new molecule or create a cool app. Unfortunately, without a great team behind that new product, it's doubtful that a great company will result.

There is an old saying that goes something like this… "I'd rather invest in an A team with a B plan than a B team with an A plan." Without a doubt, we feel this is the most important point for investors to embrace. Once you understand how critical the team is to a successful outcome, the greater success you will have as an investor. As a long term serial entrepreneur and a successful angel investor, I asked Ham to tell me how he evaluates teams and differentiates the A teams from the B teams.

Q

Ham, let's start with the person at the top. How do you evaluate startup CEOs and what are the most important characteristics you look for?

First and foremost, I look for **integrity**. That character trait might sound obvious and a bit trite, but I feel it's very important to be on alert for trust issues when you are interacting with an entrepreneur. From the initial meeting with the company, during the due diligence process, and finally while negotiating the deal, I want to make sure the CEO is being honest and negotiates in a fair manner. If I sense any duplicity at this early stage, I can be sure that things will only get worse as the company progresses through the challenges faced by all startups.

That leads me to my second character trait, **tenacity**. It's not easy being a startup CEO. The pressure to succeed is enormous, and CEOs struggle every day to motivate their team. Life in a startup is a series of highs and lows not too dissimilar from riding a roller coaster. One minute life is great as you ship your first product. The next day you hear back from customers that your product is lousy. It takes resilience to handle the good and the bad that a CEO faces on a daily basis. A CEO's tenacity allows her to continue the battle to succeed even when others would give up in despair.

Q

Okay. Those make sense, but there has to be more in the mix than that? What else do you look for?

Next on my list is a combination of **IQ and EQ**. In other words, a CEO needs to be smart and self aware. By "smart", I mean the CEO has the intelligence to discover a major market opportunity, and articulate a plan that will address that opportunity. The CEO has the intelligence to develop high-level strategic plans, and the problem solving skills to deal with day-to-day tactical and execution challenges. By "self aware", I mean the CEO works well with a great team and is willing to take guidance from close advisors. In other words, the CEO must be coachable. A great CEO wants to hire "A" team members who are better than he is for the job being filled.

> A CEO's tenacity allows her to **continue the battle to succeed** even when others would give up in despair.

A **deep market understanding** is an important skill set for a CEO because it provides the North Star from which the CEO will navigate the company. Great CEOs are two steps ahead of the competition because they have an inherent understanding of where the market is heading.

The final characteristic I look for in a CEO is **presence**. I define presence as follows... A CEO with presence has the leadership charisma to command any audience. This type of charisma allows the CEO to take charge whether speaking with employees, customers or investors. When the CEO walks into a meeting, you know who is in charge! Furthermore, this ability to command an audience gives the CEO a unique ability to create a winning culture. Building a winning company culture takes constant care and attention from the CEO, and the best way to tend to this task is by communicating a compelling story on a regular basis to the entire company.

Q

Wait - what about experience? What role does experience play in startup success?

This is a trick question, right? The obvious answer is that experience is critical. You should always back serial entrepreneurs with decades of market experience. Well… that's true in some cases. If you are looking to build the next generation of product or service in a well established market, having a few grey hairs and a deep network of contacts is probably the right way to go.

But, suppose you are trying to totally disrupt a market. For example, you are Jeff Bezos and you are looking to change the way people buy stuff. When he started Amazon, online retailing was in its infancy. Lots of market experience didn't exist. He had to make it up as time went on. So disrupting markets takes a very different type of entrepreneur. Success at Amazon had very little to do with experience and much more to do with the ability to try new things and learn as fast as possible!

Q

So you hear the CEO give her pitch and then you spend an hour or two digging into the company to learn more. How are you able to really get to know the CEO and figure out whether she has the key characteristics you are looking for?

The first step that most investors take to learn more about the CEO is to reach out and perform reference checks. Some of the references will be from contacts that the CEO provides to you. Other contacts will be people in your network that know the CEO. This type of background information is useful if you ask the right questions. At Launchpad, we have a well defined set of questions we use to guide these interviews. It helps us uncover red flag issues that we need to keep an eye out for, and it helps us apply resources to help the CEO be successful.

Personally, I find the reference checks to be useful but not sufficient in helping me get to know the CEO. I like to take things one step further. In addition to typical due diligence meetings, I arrange for time with the CEO in a non-business setting. For example, I like spending an evening with the CEO at dinner or a sporting event. Hopefully, our conversation flows smoothly with most of the discussion focused on personal topics. This way I get to know the CEO in a different context.

Q

Moving beyond the CEO, what skills do you look for in a startup company team?

There are four skills that I look for in a startup team. Given the small size of an early stage company, sometimes these skills are part of the CEO's repertoire, but I like to see them incorporated in the skill set of the other founding members.

- First, I look for **selling skills**. Whether talking to prospects, investors or future employees, the management team has to be able to sell. If you ain't sellin', nobody's buyin'!

- Second, I look for **technical skills**. I invest in tech companies and so I expect the company will have a great product that will build some competitive barriers to entry.

- Third, I look for a d**eep market awareness**. As I discussed in one of the above questions, this market awareness is critical for developing the company's strategy.

- Fourth, I look for **product management skills**. This is closely related to market awareness, because it requires the ability to listen to customers and understand the competitive environment. It also requires the ability to translate market needs into a plan that engineering can actually deliver in a timely fashion given limited company resources. Product Management is an often under appreciated skill set. A greater number of tech companies would succeed if they invested more in this critical resource.

Q

What's the right size for a startup company founding team?

It's not as though there is any magic number here, but I tend to like founding teams with 2 or 3 people. Here's my thinking on why that's the right size. To start with, we won't invest in a company that has only one person involved. If a founder can't convince a co-founder to join him in this crazy startup, why would the founder think he can convince investors to put money into the business?? With 2 co-founders, the company is moving in the right direction. Hopefully, the team has complementary skills that help round out the need for the key skills I discussed in the previous question. And, if 2 people can't pull that off, then 3 team members usually can.

Once you move up to founding teams of 4 or more you run into a lot of issues with coat-tail riders, founder dilution, outgrowing the co-founders who aren't producing, etc. Another issue to be aware of in this context is that founders always obsess about negotiating valuation and they can become overly focused on issues relating to dilution. That makes little sense when you consider the deadweight college buddy / co-founder who owns 25% of the company. Fussing about dilution by bringing in great investors and capital while having no-ops on the team, is like locking the front door but leaving the back screen door swinging in the breeze!

Chapter 10

Size Matters... How Big is Your Market?

So if we can all agree that the team is the critical factor in company success, what else do we need to look at? We believe that market opportunity and product have similar weighting in our company evaluation scale. For this chapter, I will give the nod to market opportunity and focus my questions to Christopher on what investors need to know when they evaluate a market.

As an active angel investor, Christopher looks at hundreds of companies every year. Some are tackling big problems in huge markets. Others are going after undiscovered challenges in niche markets. At first blush, most investors would choose the former investment opportunity over the latter. But you will have to dig a bit deeper to understand whether you've made the right choice. So let's see what Christopher's years of experience have done for his market sleuthing skills.

Q

Christopher, what characteristics do you think make for an interesting, investable market opportunity for startup companies?

I am looking for a market that is worth going after and offers an opportunity to build non-linear growth - very steep growth curves. By "worth going after" I basically mean big enough and durable enough over the long term (i.e. product needs which are not just a fad). By "opportunity to … grow," I am talking about market conditions which are going to allow companies to accrete value to the entity faster than they spend the entity's resources (cash/equity). In an established market, that means growing faster than the overall market growth and thereby taking market share. In a new market, that means educating and acquiring customers for less than the lifetime value of those customers.

Brand new markets are very tough to estimate in size. Your best estimate can be wildly off on both the downside or the upside. Startups routinely overestimate their markets.

Even the CEO of IBM once said the worldwide market opportunity for computers was only 5 machines. In evaluating the new market opportunity, you look for genuine pull from customers and you watch out for false demand from unsustainable marketing practices. HomeJoy is a great example of that. They raised tens of millions of dollars in venture capital and were using it to offer their $100 cleaning services through bargain sites like Groupon for $19. None of those bargain basement customers came back as repeat customers (and they all probably had really dirty houses that hadn't been cleaned in a while.)

With established markets you are looking for places where the market and the solutions on offer are kind of stuck in one way or another. These are the opportunities you can pounce on. For example…

- The market might be really fragmented with a ton of small players and it is waiting for a break-out leader,
- It might be old and calcified and totally ripe for disruption by a new entrant with a new edge, or

* It might be a really fast growing market where customers are starting to flock and can be picked off before they settle on a competitor.

One favorite situation of mine is an industry where a technical innovation or solution, such as a cloud-based market-place, is badly needed. Typically, no one particular participant in the market is going to build the solution. If they did, they would not recoup the expenses because they would build it to suit their needs only and they wouldn't want to give it to their competitors even if they could. Third parties can come into a market like this with a new and better way of doing it, and solve critical problems for everybody in the industry as a neutral and trusted third party. Salesforce.com is an example of that.

One final observation is that whatever the market, the investor syndicate must include active investors with deep experience in some aspect of the market. Maybe they have worked with these same customers in another context, or they have deep expertise with the technology, or they have built a very similar business in an adjacent space. Ideally you would have all three in the group.

> In evaluating the new market opportunity, you look for genuine pull from customers and you watch out for false demand from unsustainable marketing practices.

Q

Is there a minimum size to a potential market below which you won't invest? If so, why won't you invest?

Well, it is hard for early stage equity investors to make the numbers work with a market less than $100M in total size. It is basic arithmetic. Here is why: if early stage investors need to be able to credibly model a 10X return at the outset of every investment (because so many fail), and...

* They are only going to own part of the company, and
* The company is going to have way less than 100% market share, and
* The company is likely only going to be acquired for a revenue or EBITDA multiple of less than 10X...

Then the arithmetic won't work for much less than a $100M market.

Let's look at a couple examples. Let's say a company ends up with 5% of a billion dollar market, and the early investors put in a total of $4M in early rounds and end up holding about 12% of the company after dilution from later rounds. And let's give the company a good but reasonable revenue multiple from a buyer of, say, 7X. In that scenario, the company is worth 7 times $50M revenue (5% of a $1B market) or a total exit valuation of $350M. In that scenario, the early stage investors end up with $42M for their 12% of the $350, which is a solid 10X return.

If you run that same model with a much smaller market and no adjustments, it is a terrible result. For example let's say a company ends up with 5% of a $100M dollar market, and the early investors put in a total of $4M in early rounds and end up holding about 12% of the company after dilution from later rounds. And let's give the company the same revenue multiple from a buyer of 7X. In that scenario, the company is worth 7 times $5M in revenue or a total valuation of $35M on the company. In that scenario, the early stage investors end up with $4.2M for their 12%, which is a break-even 1X return.

What is really interesting is that if you re-run the scenario with some reasonable adjustments to reflect a lighter capitalization due to a smaller market, and a higher attainable market share percentage, you still don't get a great result. Even if you stipulate that they end up owning two times as much of the market share and you stipulate that they raise significantly less money, you are still looking at half of the desired model return.

For the sake of completeness, here's how those smaller company, smaller market numbers look. The company ends up with 10% of a $100M market (twice the market share in percentage terms than the previous example), and the early investors ended up putting $3M in ($1M less in early equity), and they end up owning 20% of the company (twice as much of the company because they were diluted less because the company raised less money). The company gets acquired for the same 7X revenue (which is probably overly generous for a market this size, if you could even find a strategic buyer for a $10M run-rate company) so they are bought for 7 times $10M or $70M, and the investors get $14M of that for their 20%. Given that they put $3M in, that is a 4.6X return.

One can play with the numbers and assumptions a bit. Put simply...

- Given the high risk of outright failure in this type of early stage investing,

- The near total lack of liquidity prior to exit,

- The amount of time it would take a start up to get 10% of a $100M market, and...

- The time it would take to find a buyer willing to pay 7X for the company,

A 1.0X - 4.6X range of best case return is much less attractive than going after a bigger market. So the $100M market probably represents the absolute floor in market size absent special circumstances.

Q

One of my pet peeves with investor presentations occurs when an entrepreneur states they are going after the $400B XYZ market, when in reality they are going after a small segment of this huge market. How do you go about determining the real size of the addressable market for a startup?

It all comes back to customer buying priorities. You can talk all you want about how big your potential addressable market is, but at the end of the day, your true market consists exclusively of those people for whom your solution is a top buying priority, plus any additional customers you can profitably convince to make it a top buying priority. It is very easy and very tempting to confuse early adopter excitement with true market pull. It has been said that "anybody can get the first 10% of a market" and Geoffrey Moore's Crossing the Chasm stands for that proposition. The key to growing a company is finding a big enough market of willing buyers who can be accessed in an affordable way (relative to their lifetime value). The product may be good, and there may be lots of people who might buy it, but unfortunately a company's true market is limited to those customers for whom that purchase is a top pain point and a top buying priority. (See the chapter on Oxygen, Aspirin & Jewelry.) Often a marginal improvement on a marginal cost is not enough to drive buying behavior in all but the earliest of adopters. So the key is to recognize when you are looking at what is sometimes called false traction and do some further digging. There is no substitute for talking to real customers and prospects before making an investment in these situations.

> You can talk all you want about how big your potential addressable market is, but at the end of the day, your true market consists exclusively of those people for whom your solution is a top buying priority.

Q

Competition plays a big role in the addressable size of the market opportunity. How do you factor the competition into your overall evaluation of the market opportunity?

Many investors look at competition as if it is the boogey-man. Sometimes you will hear about diligence efforts called off because of the discovery of unknown competitors. But there is more often another element to that kind of story, such as a lack of founder honesty or market knowledge. Experienced investors will acknowledge that competition is not bad per se. In fact, I am fond of saying "if you show me an entrepreneur with no competition, I will show you a company with no market." Even if it is just substitutes or alternatives, or other things competing for wallet share or a customer's time, everybody has some competition. And that's OK, because:

- Competitors help you bear the cost and workload of educating the market

- Their presence can legitimize and reduce the perceived risk of a new product category

- They can attract enabling services and technologies such as value-added resellers and partners and consultants with expertise

- They can attract analysts and an ecosystem around your product (such as Gartner or Forrester or other analysts recommending your product) and so on.

When competition becomes a problem it is usually when either:

- Competitors have a better value prop or a more differentiated solution (i.e. they outcompete you) or

- The market becomes so mature and so crowded that your product is commoditized and the market leaders lose pricing power. They see their margins severely compressed by lower pricing and a greater need to spend on marketing to fight to hold share.

Commoditized businesses can make money - just ask Coke and Pepsi - but the days of hyper-growth coveted by early investors are gone and not likely to come back.

What you have to do is figure out how differentiated and defensible the company's value proposition is to customers and whether it will stay compelling over the longer term. If there is pull from customers, and you can get comfortable that it is a top buying priority for an identifiable population, you are looking at a solid market opportunity.

> Experienced investors will acknowledge that competition is not bad per se. In fact, I am fond of saying "if you show me an entrepreneur with no competition, I will show you a company with no market."

- What is the landscape of potential acquirers?
- Are there big competitors looking to compete by purchasing innovative new entrants?
- Are big companies trying to buy their way into the market?
- Is the market consolidating around some key players?
- And finally, who are the likely buyers, what aspects of the business will they want, what will they be prepared to pay, and what milestones are going to need to be achieved in order to get bought?

Q

So let's say you are comfortable that the market opportunity is large enough and the team has the right product, what else should an investor determine before they write a check?

The final area to look at when considering a market is the exit options it affords. The questions I like to find answers for include:

Chapter 11

Oxygen, Aspirin or Jewelry: Which Makes a Better Investment?

Entrepreneurs fall in love with their products. It's no surprise… their product is their idea and as they nurture it, it becomes like a child to them, and who doesn't love their child!? How many times have you sat through an entrepreneur's pitch and learned practically every detail about the product, but almost nothing about the business opportunity. It's great that an entrepreneur has a great product, but what she needs to understand when dealing with investors, is that the company is the product. So a great entrepreneur makes sure she spends more time talking about the company (i.e. team, market opportunity, go-to-market strategy, finances, etc) than she spends talking about the product.

The big picture company stuff is all well and good you say, but you still need to know about the product. Will customers buy? Can the company sell the product at a profit? As a co-founder of 4 software companies, Ham spent two decades working closely with customers to understand their problems and then designed and built products to address these problems. As a former product manager, Ham gained key insights into some of the important factors that determine a product's success or failure in the market. So let's see what he does to determine if a product is smart, differentiated and defensible.

Q

Ham, what point are you trying to make for our readers with the title of this chapter?

I want our readers to think carefully about what type of product the company is building. One of Launchpad's portfolio company CEOs, Janet Kraus, was interviewed by Inc Magazine. As part of the interview, she talks about three types of business ideas: Oxygen, Aspirin and Jewelry. She goes on to explain the major aspects of each type:

- Oxygen: Products/Services that people or businesses can't live without

- Aspirin: Products/Services that reduce a major pain but are not critical to survival

- Jewelry: Products/Services that are considered luxuries and might be addictive

So which of these product types make for a better investment? Janet relates that an ideal situation is a product that has a mix of all three types. The example she gives is the iPhone which has aspects of Oxygen (e.g. email, phone), Aspirin (e.g. maps, fitness tracking) and Jewelry (e.g. games, music).

Finding a company with a product that fits all three types and is still comprehensible and good at all categories is like finding the Holy Grail of massive market opportunities. It just doesn't happen that often. So I don't recommend that investors avoid investing unless they are confident that the company has that mix. Instead, I tend to focus on finding companies with products that fall into the Oxygen category. I tend to call these "need to have" products as contrasted with "nice to have." Personally, I believe these companies make great investment opportunities, especially when risk is taken into account.

Q

Why don't you invest in Jewelry?

There is nothing wrong with luxury markets - just ask Tiffany & Co. Jewelry-like products require a different approach to investing because the customer is not a specific set of well-defined individuals you call up on the phone and talk to, it is a demographic (e.g. wealthy urban women or teenage boys). You somehow need to understand what the buying habits and interests of the broad demographic are. If you spent much of your career selling to a particular demographic, you are probably qualified to determine whether customers will buy the product. But most angel investors are not market experts with this type of experience!

To better understand the challenge you face when researching a "Jewelry" company, let's take a little test. Suppose you are thinking of investing in a new video game company. They've built an awesome new game and you and your kids really enjoy playing it. Now, ask yourself the following question: "Am I confident that 5 million American Teenage boys, ages 12 to 18, will play this game for the next 3 years?" If you can't answer this question, you should think twice about investing.

I have to admit, on occasion I invest in a "Jewelry" company. Maybe I find the CEO to be compelling, or maybe I just love the product. But, I make sure that these investments represent a very small percentage of my overall portfolio, and I accept that I am taking on greater risk because I have been unable to really verify the buying priorities.

> Is the product a 'Nice-to-Have' or a 'Need-to-Have'? As we discuss above, **Aspirin (nice-to-have) helps reduce pain but isn't critical for survival**. Whereas, you can't live without Oxygen (need-to-have).

Q

How do you go about the process of determining whether a product is "Aspirin" or "Oxygen"?

As noted above, I start with the following question: Is the product a 'Nice-to-Have' or a 'Need-to-Have'? As we discuss above, Aspirin (nice-to-have) helps reduce pain but isn't critical for survival. Whereas, you can't live without Oxygen (need-to-have).

Keep in mind that this is a continuum, and that the real difference between the two categories is just a market size question and a question about buying priorities - inevitably the Oxygen buyers are just a subset of the Aspirin buyers.

With that in mind, I reach out to current customers and prospects for the company's product. During my reference checks, I focus some of my initial questions on understanding the customer's key pain points. I ask the following two questions:

- What problem does the product solve for you?
- On your list of the top problems in your organization, where does solving this problem fall on your priority list?

By asking these two questions, you learn a lot. First of all, you hear in the customer's words what problems are solved by the product. Does that match what you are hearing from the entrepreneur in her pitch? If not, this is useful information you can pass back to the entrepreneur. If it does match, then you know the entrepreneur is doing a good job of listening to the customer.

With the answer to the second question, you are gaining critical insight helping you gauge where the product falls on the Aspirin/Oxygen spectrum. If the customer tells you that the product solves one of his top three problems, you are in Oxygen territory. Anything outside of the top 3 priorities and you are now in Aspirin territory. But don't rely on just one or two customer reference checks. This is one area where you need to dig deep during your due diligence!

Q

Okay, so the customers and prospects tell you that the entrepreneur is selling Oxygen, how do you determine if the product is differentiated and defensible?

First of all, to determine if the product is differentiated, we do a competitive analysis that combines our own research along with market outreach to customers and prospects. During our reference calls, we ask the following questions:

- How are you solving your problem today?
- Have you used similar products before?
- Did you look at any competitive products?
- Are you considering any alternative ways of solving the problem?

It's important during this stage of due diligence that you have one or two market experts helping with your research. You don't want to be blindsided by a competitor that was already very well-established in the market.

The key when looking for differentiation is to look for distinctions that matter to the customer. As we noted above, founders are in love with their product. They know every detail. They are really close to the nitty gritty - usually too close. When asked about differentiation, founders will frequently cite differences which are extremely nuanced. Even if they can even be detected by the typical hurried customer, they often will not be a major value driver from the customer's perspective. The investor's job is to figure out the differentiators that matter to the customer and make sure they are present in the product.

> **If the customer tells you that the product solves one of his top three problems, you are in Oxygen territory.**

Second, to determine if the product is defensible, we look at the question of whether hard won customers can be retained, whether pricing power will hold up and whether the margins in the business are likely to be squeezed by competitive or environmental factors. Retaining customers is all about delivering a strong value-proposition relative to your price and relative to the other things on the market. Does the company have a compelling offering?

Defending pricing and margins usually takes one of two forms: either keeping competitors out through some sort of blocking rights like intellectual property (e.g. public forms such as patents, trademarks, copyright or private forms such as trade secrets or proprietary know how), or finding ways to keep customers in. Keeping customers in requires some form of the classic economic concept of high-switching costs. In the case of Facebook, the high switching costs would be all the friends, updates, photos and data you have collected on the system and cannot figure out how to move elsewhere. On a personal computer platform it might be all the software you have invested in which is only compatible with that platform. In cameras, it might be getting someone to invest in a lot of Nikon lenses over time so they will never switch camera brands.

In case it is not obvious, businesses with high switching costs are not that easy to build, especially in today's internet-centric world where competitors' products are just a quick Google search away. More often than not, efforts to bake in switching costs just come across as product limitations which irritate consumers and slow adoption. Consumers are pretty savvy at avoiding lock-in and format wars when they can. As much as it hurts to admit it, sometimes the best lock-ins are an accident, or at least very subtle and sneaky in the beginning.

One closing thought here: "first mover advantage" is not a type of defensibility. Entrepreneurs cite it all the time, but getting an actual advantage from being a first mover is really rare and really hard.

Chapter 12

How to Apply the 3 P's to Selecting Angel Investments

The first approach we recommend for selecting investable companies is to screen each company by examining the Team, Market Opportunity and Product. That's a great way to sift through hundreds of companies to find the few diamonds in the rough. But for serious angels with more solid prospects than they can possibly invest in, a second filter is needed.

Whether they realize it or not, most investors apply a second level of filter in their screening process. Investors might use different words but they are all doing the same basic analysis. We call this secondary filter the 3 P's. They are easy to remember and understand:

1. **Potential** -- How big is the potential theoretical exit?

2. **Probability** -- How likely is the company to achieve break-out success?

3. **Period** -- How long are you likely going to have to wait?

The 3 P's are a favorite of Christopher's. He likes to discuss this filtering method when he is speaking with entrepreneurs in classes that he teaches all over the Boston entrepreneurial ecosystem. Since he challenges the entrepreneurs with answering these questions for their companies and investors, let's see how he does answering them for this chapter.

Q

We all hope for huge exits where we get more than 10x our initial investment. How do you determine the potential exit for a company?

Fantasizing about the potential is easy - after all, you can never really be proven wrong because you can just say a company didn't live up to its true potential. Predicting the objectively likely outcome is much harder. It is important to accept that you are not going to be right in many cases - that is the nature of this business.

You also need to understand the difference between strategic buyers and financial buyers. Strategic buyers purchase companies for competitive or strategic reasons, and financial buyers buy companies strictly on a "business case" basis. As a result, strategic buyers are often willing to pay more because their model for an acquisition can encompass more qualitative factors and can assume more aggressive projections due to operational synergies, investments in growth and strategic factors. Financial buyers tend to look exclusively through the lens of the net present value of future cash flows while assuming conservative growth projections and maybe a little cost-cutting.

To the extent you have a prayer of being right when determining a company's potential exit, you are going to need to start with an awareness of the strategic buyers. This requires a good sense of the ever-changing competitive landscape and the overall market of buyers of comparable companies. Questions to ask include:

- What is hot right now?
- What is cooling down?
- Where are big competitors likely to clash and feel the need to bolster their positions, or become threatened and decide to make a defensive acquisition?
- Is this company indicative of a growing trend, if it scales and succeeds?
- Who will it be stealing sales from?

In short you are asking "if my company wins, who loses or is inconvenienced or annoyed?"

Hopefully these strategic buyers are motivated by the concept of buying the entire company; perhaps for its strategic position, the threat it represents, the great brand it has built, or the number of customers or eyeballs. Sometimes strategic buyers will justify buying a company just for a single product, technology or feature. They will even sometimes buy a company for its engineers. Needless to say, the valuation goes down as you move down that list.

If your exit assumptions rely on financial buyers, you'd better go back and really look at the financial model and the operational plan. If the company's only path to market share is by burning tons of equity and there is no reliance on customer revenue to fund operations and net income to fund growth, you may be heading for a disconnect. Financial buyers are really just looking to buy the company's business and will generally value the company on a multiple of revenue, or a multiple of EBITDA. These are pretty straight-forward financial modeling exercises with pretty conservative growth, renewal and profitability assumptions. You are not often going to see financial buyers overpay using the kind of magic justifications the strategics will use.

Q

Now perhaps the hardest question: the likelihood of success. I know you don't have a crystal ball, so how do you go about measuring the probability that a company will succeed?

This one is indeed very difficult. In fact, in some ways it is easier to start by evaluating likelihood of failure. You can recognize certain problematic patterns and evaluate what they mean. If that meltdown risk feels pretty low, or there are some "soft failure" modes where you could recoup your money and maybe a small return, that can be some comfort. Turning to the success side, of course you are never going to get anywhere near certainty because so many of the companies, even in a solid angel investor portfolio, are going to fail. That is the nature of the game. But you can look at the diligence, gauge the buying priorities and resulting market size, and try to construct a mental map of a couple pathways to success. In doing so it is essential to evaluate the assumptions you are making. If the only maps you can build describe really winding routes and assume many things that just are not likely to occur, you are probably rationalizing the investment and need to be honest with yourself about the low probability. You might still choose to invest if the potential is high enough and the amount of time (and rounds) you will have to slog through before you will know is low enough, but you need to be eyes open about the lower probability of success.

> If your exit assumptions rely on financial buyers, you'd better **go back and really look** at the financial model and the operational plan.

Q

Predicting how long you will hold an investment in a startup is also not easy to do. What factors do you use to figure out approximate holding periods for your investments?

The analysis starts with who the likely buyers might be a few years out. To figure that out, you need to understand who the players might be and also understand what they are likely to buy the company for. As I mentioned above, strategic and financial buyers value companies for different reasons, so you are going to have to make some assumptions. Based on those assumptions, the next question becomes what are the milestones the company is going to need to hit before those buyers are even interested? That can be ascertained by looking at comparable deals and trying to ask around to get a sense of buying patterns in the industry. Once you have done that, the question is how long is it going to take this company to execute its plan to achieve those milestones? Here there is no substitute for experience. It always takes longer and costs more, so you should also circle back and look at the assumptions of what it is going to take and what resources are assumed in reaching those milestones. Make sure those resources will not only be available but the ultimate buyer will pay enough to deliver a good multiple on the consumed resources.

Chapter 13

Staging Capital: Angel Follow-on Theory

Most startup companies have a continuous need for funds to help grow the business. You will hear the term "Follow-on" as a frequent catchphrase for this type of investing. For example, it's common to hear one investor say to another, are you planning on "following-on" in this round? Simply put, the investor is asking if you will invest additional funds in the company.

As an early investor in a startup, you can expect to hear from the CEO when more capital is needed. There are many factors you need to examine before you make your decision. As a way of tackling this subject, I asked Ham to examine the underlying concepts behind staging investment capital in a company.

Having invested in over 30 companies and participated in more than 90 financing rounds, Ham has witnessed many different situations and evaluated companies at different times in their financing history. Participating in follow-on rounds is an important part of his approach to angel investing. Let's see if we can figure out why.

Q

Ham, tell us a bit about your philosophy for staging capital into a startup company. What's your approach?

First of all, I like to invest at a very early stage in a company's development. Typically, I invest before a product is released, and so, my initial investment is made at a very risky time in a company's lifespan. For this reason, my first check is usually quite small. It might represent as little as 25% to as much as 50% of the total I plan on investing in the company. Because the valuation of the company is typically low at this point, a smaller check still yields a meaningful chunk of stock.

By making an initial, early investment, I gain the option to invest in future rounds of the company. If the company is doing well, I might increase my ownership percentage in a follow-on round. If the company is struggling, I may still invest, but I won't put as much money in until I start to see some real progress. And in some cases, if I don't like what I see at all, I won't invest in the follow-on round. In this way, your first check is like buying an option on future rounds - you gain valuable insight and informational advantage that you can trade on as the company progresses.

When I look at my overall portfolio using the analytics built into Seraf, I see that a bit less than 50% of my invested dollars are in the first round of financing. And the remaining funds are scattered across the follow-on rounds.

> By making an initial, early investment, I gain the **option to invest in future rounds** of the company.

Q

If the valuation is so good, why don't you invest all your money in the first round of financing and be done with it?

Early seed rounds are very hard to price. The company isn't worth much because they are still early in their product development and usually have minimal revenue. So investors and entrepreneurs come up with a valuation that works for both, but that valuation is usually well above what the company is truly worth - as Christopher likes to joke: how much should you pay for two engineers, a powerpoint and a dog? As the company matures and raises additional rounds, valuations tend to approach reality. So these rounds are actually a better deal since the risk/reward ratio improves for the investor. And, because more time has passed, you are closer to exit, so even if your return multiple is lower due to the higher valuation, your IRR is higher because the money was not tied up as long.

With my initial investment, I begin closely tracking the company. I can revisit the early due diligence work we performed before our initial investment and determine whether the company is addressing the challenges as well as we expected. As an investor, you should have (or should I say - must have!) access to how the company is performing versus plan. For the top performers in your portfolio, you want to invest additional funds. As noted, you may pay a higher price than you did in the first round of financing, but your IRR is often the same or better.

Q

Why wouldn't you invest in a follow-on round?

In my case, there are two primary reasons why I don't invest in a follow-on round. I don't like investing in follow-ons where I think I am throwing good money after bad. It's not unusual for an early, seed stage investment to not pan out. These "Fail Fast on Seed Only" investments are a part of almost every angel investor's portfolio. When it is happening, you need to be honest with yourself and admit you made a mistake. There is a temptation to believe against all evidence because it is hard to throw in the towel and admit you were wrong. But that's no reason to follow-on.

The second reason is when a company is doing a very large round of financing at a big uptick in valuation. Let's say you invested in an early round where $1M bought the investors 33% of the company. Now, the company is doing great and new investors want to put $20M in for 25% of the company. My relatively small check isn't needed by the company. And, to get a reasonable multiple -- say 5x -- on this investment, the company will have to sell for at least $400M. That doesn't happen too often!

> As an investor, you should have (or should I say - must have!) access to how the company is performing versus plan. For the **top performers** in your portfolio, you want to **invest additional funds**.

Q

Are there any special cases where you stage capital in a different way?

Yes… One example is in the approach I use for investing in Life Science companies. In most cases, I invest in these companies at a very early stage in their product development. Typically, the company needs to finish product development and perform a series of clinical trials to prove the efficacy and safety of the product. Instead of raising all the capital needed to get to FDA approval, most Life Science companies raise capital over a series of 3 to 5 rounds. So, given this approach to company fund raising, I tend to invest 15-25% of the total I plan on investing in sum total into each round.

Q

What's the philosophy at Launchpad for staging capital?

With 150 members in our angel group, you should expect there will be many different philosophies for staging capital. And, you would be right! That said, Christopher and I do try to educate our angels and convince them of the value of our approach, as outlined above. We think it's important to invest early when it's relatively inexpensive but still risky. By adding our human and financial capital we can help de-risk the investment while simultaneously increasing the value of the company before subsequent rounds of financing.

"But," you say, "as a smart investor, I will wait until you've improved the risk/reward ratio to the point where I can step in and write a big check!" Well, that approach will work sometimes, but not always. And often the times it doesn't work are precisely the companies where you most want it to. At Launchpad, two of our best investments are companies that raised their first round of financing from us, and then, proceeded to take off. When new investors came in for the Series B round of financing, they didn't allow other new investors to participate. If you didn't invest in the first round, you were locked out of the investment. So keep that in mind when you are mulling over making that early stage investment… you just might want to write a small check to gain a seat at the table!

Chapter 14

Convertible Notes: Good or Evil?

One of the most controversial topics in the startup community relates to the issue of investing through convertible notes vs. investing through preferred stock. Much has been written about this topic for the past decade, and the debate continues to rage in the blogosphere even today.

Even though this topic has been covered by others, we felt it was important to give our perspective. We've done hundreds of investments, many using Convertible Notes. So our viewpoint is a practical viewpoint and not an academic one. We live this issue every day and do our best to steer through the minefield and avoid as many mines as possible.

Q

Christopher, tell us a bit about the history of convertible notes. How did they get started in the first place?

It is my understanding that convertible notes first came into use in the startup space in the context of quick bridge rounds by VCs who had already given a term sheet to a company. They were a quick and simple way to funnel a little interim working capital into a company while an investing syndicate for a priced round was being built, papered and funded. Notably, in this scenario there isn't much pricing risk to allocate between the buyer and seller since the price of the coming round has already been set. Convertible notes made decent sense in this context, but somehow they escaped and metastasized into a general purpose financing tool and are currently used in places where they don't make as much sense.

Q

So let's start with situations where you think convertible notes make the most sense. Why would you recommend a convertible note? What are the pros for investors and for entrepreneurs?

There are two places where they make sense: very small initial seed rounds and supplemental bridges between priced rounds. Here's why. The main things convertible notes have going for them are:

- They are cheaper to put together because there are fewer legal documents and they are simpler

- They are less complex and have fewer variables to negotiate, particularly deal price which is a perennially thorny topic that entrepreneurs like to postpone settling if they can and

- They are not an issuance of stock, so they don't require a single big coordinated legal closing to re-capitalize the company and revise the charter the way a stock deal does.

This means that super early-stage entrepreneurs can try to close individual investors one at a time on a rolling basis, and it means that they can do much smaller rounds without the transaction cost getting too high as a percentage of the round.

These advantages are all great for the entrepreneur. Unfortunately, none of them are really advantages for investors - all of the things being scuttled in the name of speed, simplicity and cheapness are basically investor protections, or at least more granular ways of allocating risk and reward.

> By investing early they are **helping the company** get up the really steep part of the valuation curve, and so they ought to benefit from the chance to **share with the entrepreneur** in that upside they helped create.

Q

Okay, now let's discuss the cons. What makes notes so reviled by angel investors? And why wouldn't an entrepreneur want to use a note?

The fundamental problem is misalignment between the investor and the entrepreneur on price. In a note, the price of the stock you will get is not set at the time you commit - it will be set at a future time in connection with a future priced round. So if the price on that future round is set high, the entrepreneur wins and gives less stock to the note holders. If the price is set low, the investors win and get more stock for their original investment. Your investors win if you lose. Not a great set of incentives for your investors.

There are a number of ways to address the issue by putting a cap or maximum price at which note holders will convert, and/or promising them an automatic discount on the price of the round, or even giving them some warrants instead of a discount. These mechanisms don't really solve the problem, and introduce their own set of issues. The cap has the effect of pricing the round (or at least sending a strong price signal) in the eyes of the market, so if the entrepreneur sets the cap high, they are fencing themselves into a high implied valuation that they may not be ready for when the day comes. And if they set it low, they are going to experience a lot of dilution if the round prices a lot higher than the cap and suffer a mounting "note overhang." They don't like that, and future investors don't like that, which creates an incentive to renegotiate the terms of the note, which naturally leads to chaos and animosity all around.

All this is happening at a time when the company is really risky and its theoretical value/valuation is changing extremely rapidly with each step along the progress path. A lot of investors feel that equity upside is the perfect compensation for taking all that early risk on. By investing early they are helping the company get up the really steep part of the valuation curve, and so they ought to benefit from the chance to share with the entrepreneur in that upside they helped create. If you give up that upside by doing a note, the investors are basically taking equity risk for debt returns.

Note holders are also taking on the risk that their contractual terms can be renegotiated at any time (as contrasted with the harder-to-alter rights you get as a holder of equity). Different batches of notes with different caps can pile up and it can be a mess to figure out how to reconcile them and actually figure out the exact price of the different notes while trying to give effect to multiple notes at once. This pits note-holders against note-holders. Enter later investors, who know that note terms can be changed, so they can just condition their investment on giving the note holders a haircut and cleaning everything up. Since this type of haircut doesn't hit the founders in the wallet the way, say, imposing a recap on all early equity holders would, the founders are economically incentivized to go along with the suggestion, putting them once again at odds with their early investors.

And finally, it must be observed that note holders also have none of the other protections like board seats, protective provisions, a minimum needed for the round to close, pro-rata rights, drag along rights, registration rights, etc. It is true that you can come up with mechanisms such as note-holders' agreements, investor rights agreements, voting agreements, side letters, etc. to put any of those features back in, but by the time you have done a capped note with a discount and a bunch of other bells and whistles, you have destroyed the greatest virtue of notes - their cheap simplicity - and yet you still have an awkward transaction compared to a proper priced round.

So at the end of the day, convertible notes (and other deferred pricing structures like SAFEs) are not good for investors and they are also not ideal for entrepreneurs. Their defects tend to get over-looked in very small rounds because they are a cheap and easy transaction to do. But if you just want a cheap transaction with few protections, I'd suggest it would be better to just buy some common stock - you might find better alignment with your founders that way.

Q

I expect the debate around the merits of Convertible Notes will continue to rage for years to come. Any last parting thoughts you would like to lay out on the table?

Yes. Believe it or not I have just skimmed the surface of this issue and talked about the most basic issues. There are actually quite a few more subtle legal and economic issues involved with notes, each of which have the potential to be equally important, especially for entrepreneurs. For people seeking more detail, I recommend some great writing by VC Mark Suster on this topic as well as some of the other pieces he links to.

Notes are just not a good way to invest and it is really a shame that they have become a market standard and the only way a lot of rounds can get done.

Chapter 15

Key US Federal Tax Issues for Angel Investors

As we all know, the United States IRS tax code is extremely complex. Because the code includes some provisions directly affecting angel investing, understanding the tax rules is important for US-based angel investors. There are significant tax savings for angel investors who understand the rules. In addition, there are some tax rules that could cost you if you don't understand what you are getting into.

A full vetting of all the angel tax issues is beyond the scope of this chapter, but we will give you a high level overview of issues to be cognizant of. Furthermore, IRS tax rules are in a constant state of flux. This chapter will discuss the rules as of the date of this book. We can't recommend strongly enough that you hire an accountant who understands the tax rules for investments in Qualified Small Business Stock (QSBS).

- Acquired between 8/10/1993 and 2/17/2009:   50% Exclusion

- Acquired between 2/18/2009 and 9/27/2010:   75% Exclusion

- Acquired between 9/28/2010 and 12/31/2016:   100% Exclusion

We don't know whether or how this tax benefit will be applied in the future. The US Congress tends to decide on these types of tax provisions on annual basis.

Q

Ham, let's start with our favorite section in the IRS tax code. What can you tell us about Section 1202?

By far the biggest tax benefit for US investors in early stage companies falls under IRS Tax Code Section 1202. This tax provision allows for the exclusion of up to 100% of your capital gains for your US Federal taxes. As long as you hold your stock for a minimum of 5 years before the sale occurs, your capital gains exclusion is calculated as follows:

Q

There's another section that is useful to know about when you have a winning exit. What's the deal with Section 1045?

Many of you are familiar with the fact that you can reduce the amount of taxes on your capital gain from selling your primary residence as long as you purchase a new home within 24 months of the sale of your original home. There is a similar "rollover" provision for QSBS investments called Section 1045.

This provision allows you to avoid paying any capital gains as long as you put all of your gains into a new QSBS investment within 60 days. Furthermore, the holding period of the replacement stock includes the holding period of the stock you just sold. This is a great way to help you get the preferential tax treatment of Section 1202 for your long term capital gains. But be careful… don't let the tax tail wag the investment dog. The 60 day window is very short, so you shouldn't jump into a new investment just to save on your taxes. That's a great way to turn those gains into a big loss!

Q

I had a big loss in my portfolio last year. Are there any tax benefits that I should be aware of?

It's never fun writing off one of your investments, but it happens about half the time in a portfolio of early stage investments. In the worst case scenario, you can write off your losses vs. any capital gains you receive in the calendar year. But there is a provision in the tax code, called Section 1244, that allows you to write off your losses vs. the higher earned income tax rate. That can make a big difference since capital gains are taxed around 20% and earned income rates can be as high as 39%.

In order to take advantage of Section 1244, your investment must be part of the initial $1M invested in a QSBS company. It's important to document and track the fact that you qualify as early as you can. Seraf helps you with this tracking by: 1) asking when you record a new investment whether it's 1244 qualified and 2) allowing you to store any documents you might have to prove that your investment was 1244 qualified in case your tax returns are audited.

> Section 1202. This tax provision allows for the **exclusion of up to 100% of your capital gains** for your US Federal taxes.

Q

Are there any tax issues investors should be aware of when they invest in Convertible Notes?

Yes, there are! There are three areas you need to be aware of.

1. You may have to recognize, and pay tax on, interest payments accruing on your note even though you didn't receive any cash payments from the company.

2. In most cases, no capital gain is recognized when the note is converted to stock, but the conversion of the note does trigger interest income recognition even if the interest is paid in stock vs. cash.

3. Be careful when warrants are issued along with the convertible note. The value assigned to the warrants has the effect of creating a discount on the note (since the warrants have to have some value and you are paying the same as other note holders not getting warrants), and therefore, some income reporting associated with the imputed income of getting a note below fair market value.

So, make sure you have an accountant who understands the complexities of QSBS investments. You want to make sure you don't get tripped up by an IRS audit!

Chapter 16

Stock Warrants: Sweetening the Deal for Angel Investors

One of the less understood and seldom used instruments in angel investing is the stock warrant. Warrants are essentially the same as the more familiar stock option. Both are a contractual right to buy a certain amount of stock at some point in the future, at a price agreed upon now. In effect, both are a pure upside play with no downside risk prior to exercise. The two names are simply associated with different contexts.

Q

Christopher, what are warrants? How are they different from options?

Options are typically given to employees, often pursuant to a defined option plan which sets out many of their terms. Options used in the employee compensation context are often eligible for preferential tax treatment. By contrast, warrants are more typically used in the context of transactions with third parties (investors, vendors, bankers, partners, etc. rather than employees.) They typically have all their terms built right in the warrant document rather than in a separate plan. This means warrants are generally one-offs that do not draw down any pre-approved pool of shares set aside (the way options do). And, while they can be exercised and held in a way that gets you capital gains, it is not as easy as with incentive stock options that are given to employees in connection with a qualified stock option plan.

In our experience, the most common use for warrants is when they are used as a "deal sweetener" to convince angel investors to invest sooner rather than later in a new round of financing, and they are sometimes used instead of a discount to make convertible notes perform more like equity.

Q

Why should an angel investor be interested in having stock warrants as part of an investment deal?

Warrants are prized by investors because they give you upside appreciation rights without requiring you to commit any capital. You get a locked-in price at which you can buy any time (i.e., your strike price), but you don't have to buy (i.e., exercise your warrants) unless the stock price goes above your strike price. You get the benefit of a winner without the risk of committing the associated capital.

Q

When is the 'right' time to exercise your warrants?

Generally speaking the best strategy for exercising warrants is to wait until you are sure the company is totally out of the woods (and the warrants will therefore definitely be worth something) and then, once you have made that determination, exercise them as soon as possible to start the capital gains clock running so it hopefully has at least a year to run before any acquisition occurs. That way they are treated as long term capital gains with a preferential rate, as opposed to short term capital gains, which are taxed at the same rate as ordinary income. Put another way, you want to exercise them as soon as you reach the point that you are sure you are going to exercise them. Bit of a tautology, and most people just set them aside until the last possible minute and then exercise them as late as possible. Can be a fine strategy IF you are able to hold the stock for a year. If the company gets bought after you exercise, you can be looking at higher taxes that were avoidable if you had known for the last several years you were going to exercise them.

Q

So why not just exercise them right away?

Because you have to spend money to exercise them. If the exercise price is fair market value (FMV) at the time they are granted, that can be real money - equivalent to simply investing in the company at that price. True, if the warrants are issued way below FMV, say for a penny each, then you might as well exercise them right away, because it costs you next to nothing to do it. But if they are issued at FMV, and FMV is a buck or two a share, it would cost money to exercise them. Unless you know the company is going somewhere for sure, why pay for what would otherwise be a free chance to wait and see?

> In our experience, the **most common use for warrants** is when they are used as a "deal sweetener" to convince angel investors to **invest sooner rather than later** in a new round of financing.

Q

In most cases, warrants have a void date 5 to 10 years in the future. How do you keep track of your warrants so you don't forget to exercise them when the opportunity is right?

Ah, here is the wellspring from which all warrant misery flows. Warrants expire and many people forget about the expiration date. Even if the company remembers, it is under no obligation to tell you (in fact, it already told you, right on the face of the warrant under the clause about expiration date!) Many experienced angels with a lot going on in their portfolio outright forget they even have warrants in a deal, let alone which round they are associated with and when they expire. When we were building and market-testing Seraf, we heard many tales of woe about forgotten warrants. Even if you put them in a calendar, you can forget - who keeps the same paper or electronic calendar system for 10 years?

So we knew we needed to build a robust date tracking system into Seraf that not only allows you to see all your key dates, it allows you to set custom reminders to alert you in advance of any key dates you choose. So, for example, when I get warrants, I always note the ultimate expiration date but I also set reminders to myself to check on them and see if it is time to exercise them. Nailing a profitable exercise of a pile of "in the money" warrants you would have otherwise totally forgotten about can pay the lifetime price of Seraf hundreds of times over!

Chapter 17

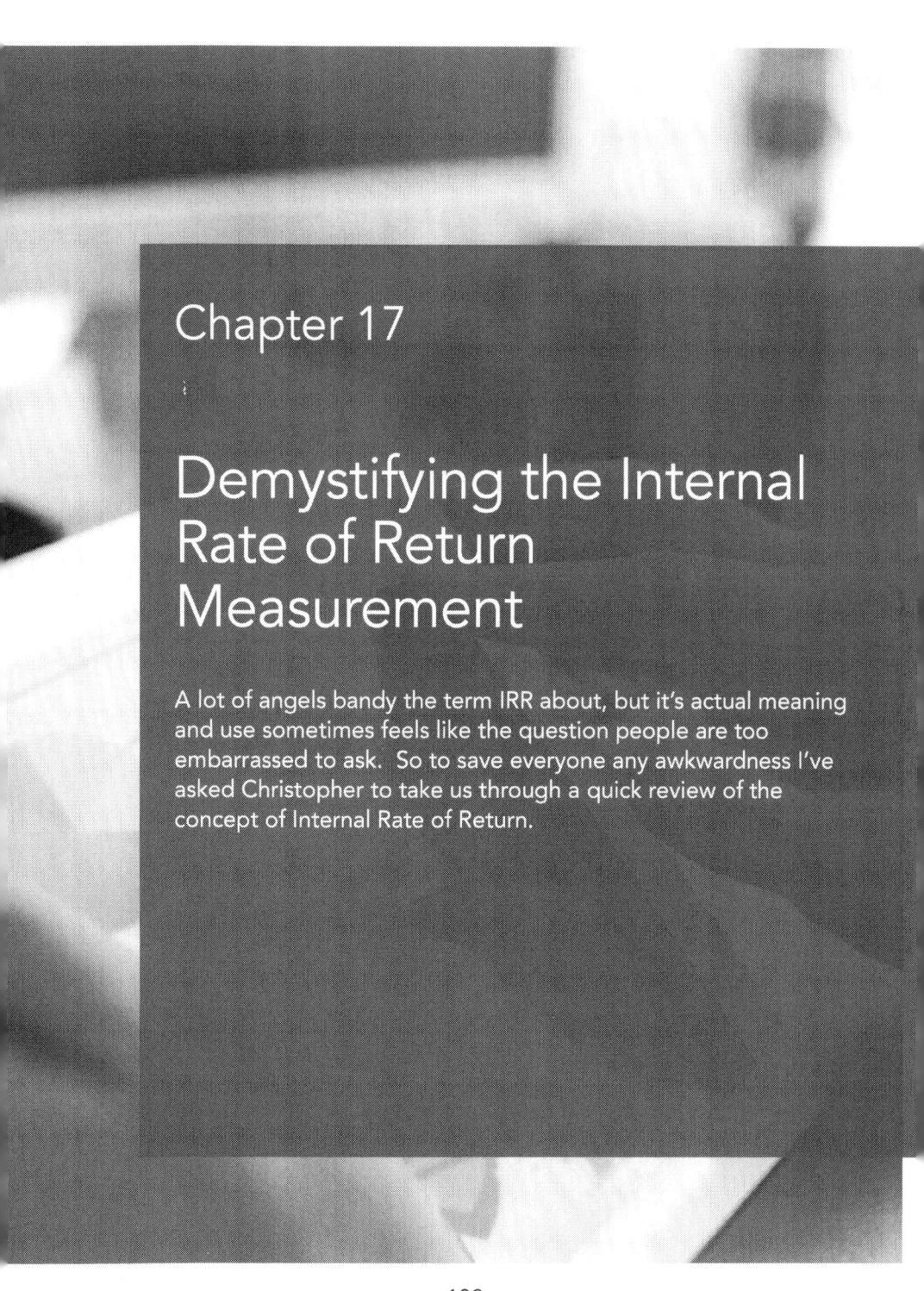

Demystifying the Internal Rate of Return Measurement

A lot of angels bandy the term IRR about, but it's actual meaning and use sometimes feels like the question people are too embarrassed to ask. So to save everyone any awkwardness I've asked Christopher to take us through a quick review of the concept of Internal Rate of Return.

Q

What does IRR stand for?

IRR stands for "internal rate of return" and is a more complicated way of looking at your returns which takes elapsed time into account as one of the factors. It is actually a concept that originated in the bond markets and was adopted by corporate finance professionals in the large enterprise context for planning capital budgeting (and in that context is sometimes called the discounted cash flow rate of return). Pure finance theory says the project with the higher IRR should be prioritized over the project with the lower IRR. Closed-end funds such as a typical venture capital fund have adopted IRR for their own purposes as a standard measure of performance, and so, as with many other things, angels have inherited the IRR habit from VCs. In the context of a patient angel who does not have to repay limited partners at a fixed point in time (e.g. the end of a ten year fund), IRR may be less meaningful than a simple exit multiple, but Seraf includes it because many investors find it helpful.

Q

Is IRR important? If so, why?

IRR is not important, per se. It is just one way of looking at your investments which is a bit more complicated than exit multiple, because IRR takes that element of elapsed time into account. Think of it as a harsher grade for your investments. If you think in pure exit multiples, then you are inclined to think of your investments as having overly rosy returns. A 2X is "wow, 200% return!" A 2X in 6 years is an IRR of 12.2%. Not quite as rosy because your money was tied up a pretty long time and bore a fair amount of risk to merely double. (And if you really want to grade yourself harshly, subtract the nominal returns the money would have gotten in your favorite market index. The net after that subtraction is the true internal rate of return you earned over what you would have otherwise.)

> In the context of a patient angel who does not have to repay limited partners at a fixed point in time (e.g. the end of a ten year fund), IRR may be less meaningful than a simple exit multiple.

Q

How are Exit Multiple and IRR calculated?

Exit multiple is a very simple calculation. It is the total cash out divided by the total cash in. So if you put $50,000 in and got $150,000 back, your exit multiple would be 3X.

To calculate IRR, think of it as follows: the internal rate of return on an investment is the annualized effective compounded return rate that would be required to make the net present value of the investment's cash flows (whether they be cash in or cash out) equal out to a perfect ZERO. The actual equation is sometimes expressed like this: NPV = NET*1/(1+IRR)^year. IRR can also be thought of as that particular discount rate at which the present value of future cash flows become equal to the original investment (or put another way, the rate of return necessary for the investment to break even). In the investment context, the IRR of your investment is the discount rate at which the net present value of your investment's costs (the negative cash flows) is equal to the net present value of your investment's returns (the positive cash flows).

Q

Why do the Exit Multiples and IRRs vary so much from round to round in a single company?

The variation is entirely due to the time element. A second investment round immediately prior to the sale of the company, which as a result generates a return almost immediately, can have a much higher IRR than an earlier investment, even if the earlier investment was at a much lower valuation and had a higher exit multiple. This illustrates the time element of the IRR calculation - finance theory punishes projects which tie up cash longer.

Chapter 18

Early Stage Investment Syndication: Key Issues

A very common practice in the investment world is syndication. Syndication allows multiple investors -- whether they be individuals, angel groups, VC funds, etc. -- to join together and provide the funding resources needed by one company. Syndication has been a common practice amongst VC firms for decades. It's also been common practice amongst individual angel investors who have increasingly chosen to come together into angel investment groups. As of very recently, the term is used by some of the on-line platforms to connote a mechanism whereby a group of investors can commit money to be invested alongside a lead investor. But for the purposes of this discussion we are focused on syndication between angel groups.

Inter-group syndication of this type has only been common for about ten years in the angel group world. It makes a lot of sense because it broadens both the financial and the human capital resource base of the company, but it is a challenge because it requires a fair amount of coordination amongst a lot of people.

Some of the very first syndicates were formed in New England in the mid-2000s. Given the close geographic proximity between angel groups in the Northeast, it was natural for these groups to band together and pull together large financings for startup companies.

Ham, in his position as Managing Director at Launchpad Venture Group, played a big role in some of the first angel group syndicates in New England. So let's hear what he has to say about how angels can work together to form enough capital to properly launch a startup company.

Q

Ham, tell us about one of the early angel group syndicates you were involved with.

In April 2005, Launchpad was introduced to a very promising Medical Diagnostics company called Cognoptix. The company was developing a new approach for the early detection of Alzheimer's. Their technology was a real breakthrough in an area of growing concern and significant costs to the US Healthcare system. We were impressed with the founding team and knew this was a company we wanted to back. As is typical with early stage life science companies, Cognoptix expected to raise significant money before they would be ready for an acquisition. When they approached us in 2005, they were looking for a relatively small amount of capital, in the neighborhood of $1M, to help them take their proof of concept to the next stage. After completing our due diligence over the spring months, we were ready to move forward with an investment. However, Launchpad was a relatively small angel group at the time, and we didn't have enough capital from our members to fully fund Cognoptix.

During this same time period, the Managing Directors of angel groups throughout the New England region were meeting on a monthly basis to discuss best practices at our respective groups. One area of focus during our meetings was figuring out ways of raising larger amounts of capital for early stage companies in our portfolios. George McQuilken, the Managing Director at eCoast Angels, offered to hold a regional angel group meeting in Portsmouth, NH. One of the main agenda items at the meeting was a series of investor presentations by companies looking to fill out an open round of financing. Launchpad invited Cognoptix to present to the audience of approximately 100 angel investors. With a term sheet in hand and an endorsement by Launchpad, Cognoptix was able to raise the rest of their open round within 2 weeks of their presentation. Angels from groups all over New England participated in the initial round and continued to fund the company in several subsequent rounds of financing. This was the first large multi-angel group syndicate formed in the US.

> Helping a company raise funds with a syndicate of investors **adds time and complexity to the fundraising process**, and you will need to take this into account when you are helping an entrepreneur raise capital.

Q

What are some of the biggest challenges in putting together a syndicate?

Pulling together a syndicate of investors is never easy, whether you are talking about individual angels, angel groups, or VCs. Helping a company raise funds with a syndicate of investors adds time and complexity to the fundraising process, and you will need to take this into account when you are helping an entrepreneur raise capital. First off, you have to find a lead investor to negotiate the deal terms with the entrepreneur and then manage the syndicate of investors. It's common to hear an entrepreneur lament the fact that they have lots of interested investors lined up if only they could find someone to lead the deal. Assuming that the lead investor is on board and willing to help with the fund raising, there remain additional challenges.

Let's take a look at some of the bigger issues we faced at Launchpad in the dozens of deals we syndicated over the past 10 years. As mentioned above, it takes a lot of time to syndicate a deal. As the lead investor, after negotiating a termsheet and preparing a syndication-worthy diligence report, you are expected to:

- Work with the company to determine the minimum amount of financing needed to help the company achieve key future funding milestones
- Build a fundraising plan to hit the target amount of needed financing
- Introduce the entrepreneur to potential investors and investor organizations
- Support and champion the deal with potential investors
- Share your diligence materials with potential investors and be available to answer questions about your diligence process and findings
- And finally, work to make sure the deal closes in a timely fashion

Do all syndicate leaders take on all of these activities? No... but the good ones do, and they make a big difference in a company's ability to raise capital.

Q

What are some important issues that investors need to be wary of?

When you are asked to join a syndicate of investors, you should be careful about how much you rely on the lead investor's ability to properly perform due diligence on the company. Especially with angel investors, there is a broad range of approaches to diligence and in such a range, there will always be some approaches that do not live up to your personal standards. And, in some cases, even when there has been some good diligence work done, you might still be asked to invest without any written diligence report from that effort. Here's a tip: if you have a certain set of diligence standards that you apply before you make an investment decision, don't give up on those standards just because you are impressed by your co-investors.

Another challenge with syndicated deals relates to investor alignment. What do I mean by "investor alignment"? When you have multiple investors in a company, you want to make sure they are in agreement as to:

- The best path to exit for the company, and
- What an acceptable exit would be

For example, if you have angel investors who would be happy with a 3x return in a year or two and a VC who is looking for a 10x return in three to five years, you might have an alignment issue. If the VC has voting control on the board, she can block an exit that might be acceptable to the angel investors. I've been in this situation before, and in the end, the company was sold for pennies on the dollar instead of the 3x return that the VC rejected. That's the hard way to learn the alignment lesson! So, it's important to know your co-investors and what their expectations are for the company.

Q

What are some important issues that entrepreneurs need to be wary of?

From the entrepreneur's perspective, there are a variety of factors that need to be taken into consideration when building an investor syndicate. Investor alignment, as we discussed in the previous question, is a key consideration. For example, you want to make sure, before you finalize an investment, that the founders and the investors are on the same page with respect to fundraising strategy. Other issues to consider include:

- Make sure the lead investor knows how to champion a deal and has great connections to other investors.
- Build a syndicate with angels and other investors who will add value by making connections, helping find future key hires, and in general opening their personal network to help the company.
- Coach the CEO and board appointees on how to run an organized and efficient syndicate, including not trying to get too many irons in the fire at once.
- Be very wary of the investor who is constantly pestering you for information, and never adds any value to the company.
- The list can go on and on…

Chapter 19

Timing Is Everything: Angel Investing Success

Ask a great investor what factors are most critical in his/her success in selecting investments and you will probably hear some variation on the following list: 1) Great Team, 2) Great Idea, 3) Huge Market Opportunity and 4) Innovative Business Model...

When we evaluate companies, as you have read in past chapters, we spend a lot of time analyzing these factors. And that's because they are critically important. But there is one other factor that most people don't think about and very few track.

So what is this key factor?? It's Timing!

Not what you were expecting, was it? Let's take you through it and, we expect you will understand why you need to consider timing as part of your overall investment planning.

Q

Ham, start us out here. Please be more specific about what you mean by timing?

I look at the issue of timing and ask two questions when I think about making an investment. First, I ask the timing question:

Is this the right time for this idea?

There is a lot of nuance in this question. It could mean that the world is not ready for it. For example, way back in 1994, Time Warner teamed up with Silicon Graphics to build a video-on-demand service in Orlando, Florida. Unfortunately, this project failed miserably. There were issues around high costs, difficulties with network infrastructure, and on and on. Does that mean it was a terrible idea? Of course not: fast forward 15 years and you are surrounded by fast-growing video on demand services.

> You **don't have any control** over what goes on with the economy. So what can you do as an investor to make sure you don't end up losing it all due to bad timing? Here's where a **different type of diversification** kicks in

What accounts for the difference? Timing. All of the blocking issues went away because of the availability and reduced cost of leveraging high speed broadband throughout most of the world. Companies like Netflix are huge businesses today because people want video-on-demand and they can purchase a great product at a reasonable price.

Another way to parse this question would be to ask if the company is too late. For instance, we all know that Google wasn't the first search engine. Yahoo, Infoseek and AltaVista are a few of the many search engines that were available years before Google came to market. Google ended up dominating the market. So Google wasn't too late because it was still a developing market. But obviously, that window of opportunity starts to close at some point. Today, if you want to build a new search engine, it's going to be very difficult to get traction and take away significant market share from Google.

The second timing question I ask when making an investment is:

When do I expect this investment to mature and reach an exit?

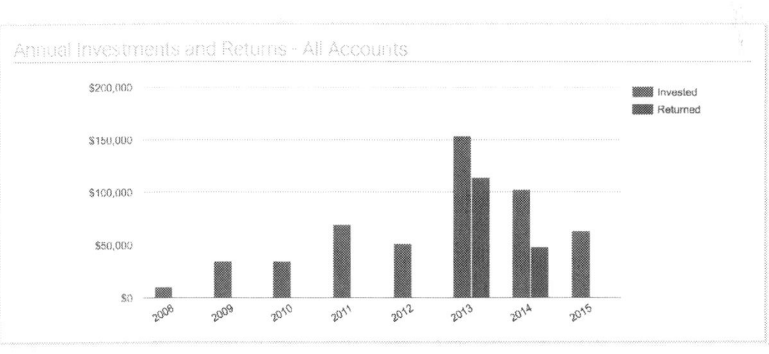

This timing question relates less to what is going on in a specific industry, and more to what's going on in the broader economy and the stock market. Imagine you are an investor in 1999 and you are invested in larger faster-growing internet companies that were experiencing significant traction. Your timing is great - the IPO market was red hot, so you could exit your investments and make a ton of money. Now, imagine you are an investor in 1999 and you are making your initial investments into young startup companies. Your timing is awful! The dotcom bubble burst in 2000 and most of your investments went to zero. VCs who raised new funds in 1996 and 1997 made a killing. Those who raised new funds in 1999 and 2000 went bust.

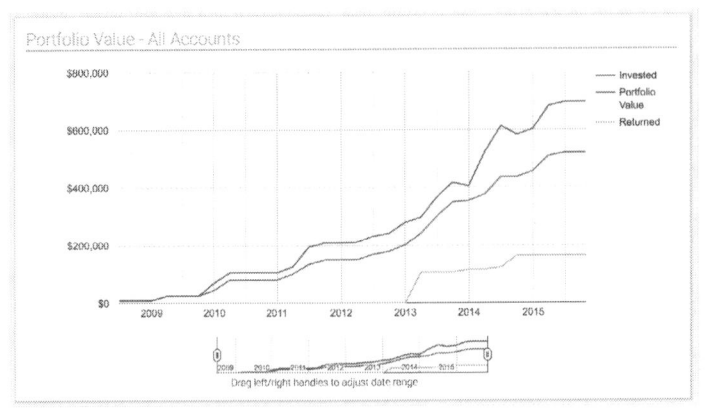

You don't have any control over what goes on with the economy or the stock market. So what can you do as an investor to make sure you don't end up losing it all due to bad timing? Here's where a different type of diversification kicks in. If you look at your portfolio and plot out when you think your investments will exit, does it cluster around a short timeframe? Are they all trendy "it" companies of the moment which are raising inflated rounds at inflated prices? If so, you need to diversify in a different way by adding investments that will build value more slowly based on fundamentals and exit over a broader time period. If you invest in 20 or more companies and you make your investments at a steady pace of 2 to 4 new companies per year, you should have built-in timing diversification. That said, it's a useful exercise to revisit your portfolio and examine when you think exits are most likely given the progress made by each company.

Q

Since we need to track timing as part of our overall portfolio diversification, how do we do it?

You need to have some way of organizing your angel investment portfolio. You should know exactly how many investments you have, when you made those investments and how well the investments are doing. Keeping all this information in one, well organized location sounds daunting, but it doesn't have to be. It's the main reason we developed

Seraf, and I use it to manage my personal angel portfolio and to track the Launchpad Venture Group portfolio.

With simple charts like these, you have a sense for when you've made your investments, and are able to see whether they are spread out over time or clustered in short time periods.

Overlay that information with an understanding of how much progress your investments are making, and you will get a sense for how many companies might exit in the near and mid-term. Too many exits focused on a short period of time adds risk to your portfolio.

Obviously there is an element of luck because the economic cycle is not something you can really time, but when building a diverse portfolio and assuring that your personal "evergreen angel fund" will have enough liquidity to invest over the long-haul, you need to make sure that likely time of "peak ripeness" is one of the elements you pay attention too. An angel portfolio consisting entirely of really long term moonshots is going to require a lot of capital before it returns a dime. Mixing some likely early exits in is not only going to provide you with some early capital returns, it is a lot more fun!

Section Three

Understanding Early-Stage Deal Terms

We live in a world where you can buy stocks in publicly traded companies at the click of a button. Purchasing 100 shares of Apple is easier than purchasing a bottle of wine at your local wine merchant. Maybe some day in the future purchasing stock in an early stage, private company will be just as easy.

But today, we are a long way from having private company stock transactions this streamlined. Each private deal is custom-crafted, and it takes considerable time and energy to negotiate the deal and produce the investment documents.

The **Term Sheet** is the document that starts it all. Crafting a term sheet is how most of the real negotiation between investor and company occurs. It can be a challenge to properly account for and allocate the many risks and benefits in an early stage deal. So both sides of the table need to know what terms do which things. It's also very helpful if the attorneys on both the investor and company side are experienced in drafting these types of investment documents.

This section on Term Sheets and Deal Documents will outline key concepts you should master so you will become a better, more informed investor. You will learn the following:

- What are the four key subject matter areas in a term sheet
- When negotiating a term sheet, what are the biggest concerns for investors and what are the biggest concerns for founders
- Which deal terms will have the biggest impact on your financial outcomes
- Which deal terms provide you with a say in critical business decisions for the company
- Besides the Term Sheet, what documents will you see as part of your investment

Having negotiated over 100 early stage investment term sheets, we are able to cut through the clutter of dense legal documents. We expressly designed this section as a practical outline for investors and not a treatise for law students or first year associates.

So read on... and learn how experienced investors think about and structure their deals.

Chapter 20

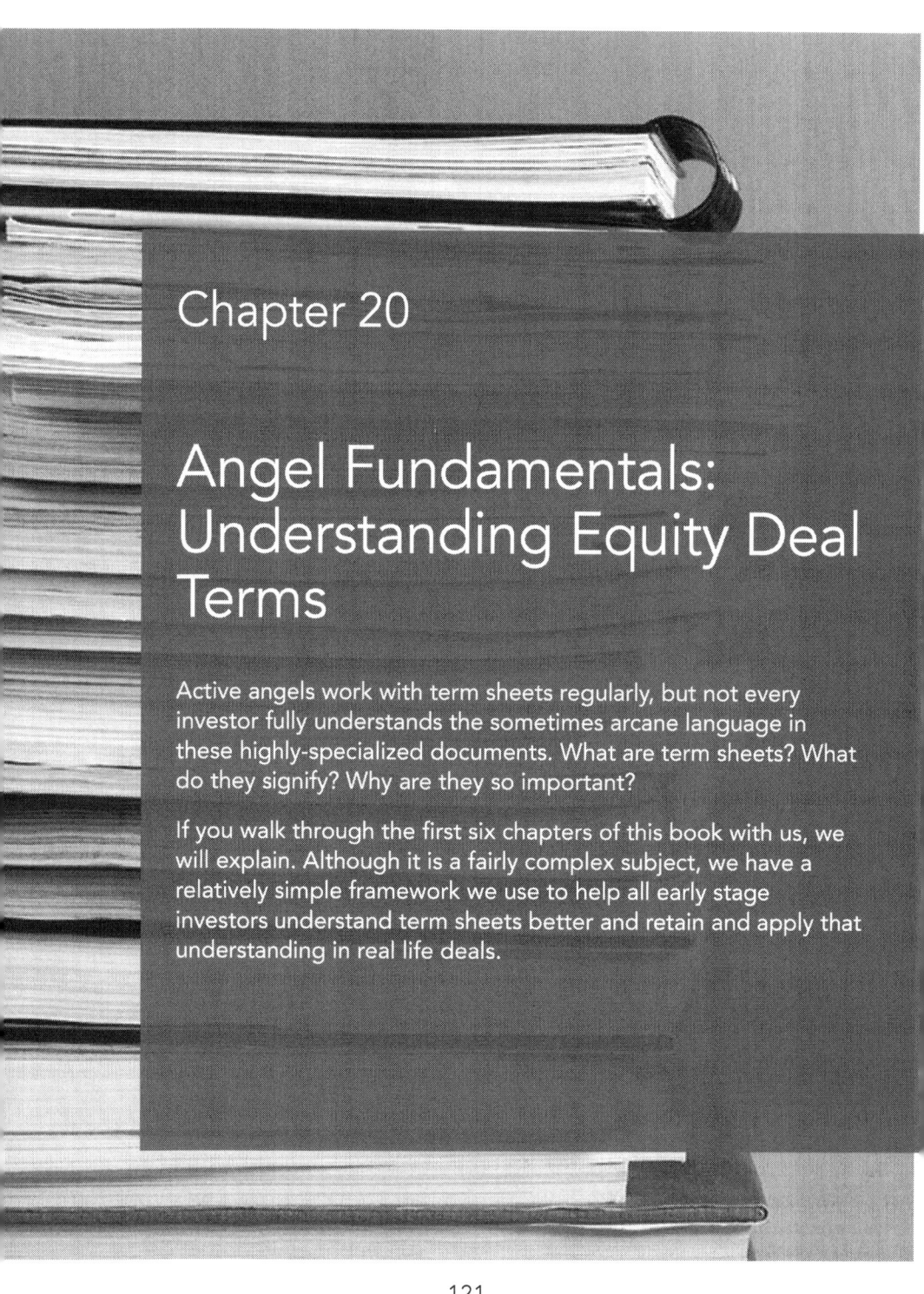

Angel Fundamentals: Understanding Equity Deal Terms

Active angels work with term sheets regularly, but not every investor fully understands the sometimes arcane language in these highly-specialized documents. What are term sheets? What do they signify? Why are they so important?

If you walk through the first six chapters of this book with us, we will explain. Although it is a fairly complex subject, we have a relatively simple framework we use to help all early stage investors understand term sheets better and retain and apply that understanding in real life deals.

Non-Binding; Summary Instructions

Most early-stage investments start with or are accompanied by a "term sheet" summarizing the terms of the deal. Unless a term sheet expressly states that it contains legally binding sections, early stage investment term sheets are not legally binding agreements. Instead, term sheets can be thought of more like a set of notes outlining the principal elements of the deal as agreed by the negotiating parties. They serve as a basis for soliciting interest from prospective investors as well as a guide for use by counsel drafting up the definitive binding documents.

The problem is that they can be dense and complex. Term sheets can cover literally dozens of subjects. They are written in very jargon-heavy shorthand so they can be quite intimidating for less-experienced investors. You will see provisions on everything from price, size of round, composition of the board to liquidation preferences, and anti-dilution protection.

Management & Control

Investors want to know what's going on in the company, have a say in decisions, and want to control founder behavior to avoid damaging company

Exits & Liquidity

Investors want to make sure they can get their money back in all possible scenarios, even if they have to force it

Protection

Investors want to make sure nobody diminishes the value of their investment or gets liquidity ahead of them

Deal Economics

Investors want to make sure they get a big enough slice of the pie, want to make sure they get paid back first, want to put a time-clock on the founders, and want to make sure employee options don't dilute them

Framework: Four Key Areas of Concern

But these documents do not need to be overwhelming because all term sheet issues can be grouped into four basic areas. Within those areas, the individual provisions can be thought of as a group of tools representing a negotiated balancing or risk allocation between the concerns of the founders and the concerns of the investors. So what are those four key areas?

- Deal Economics
- Investor Rights / Protection
- Governance, Management & Control
- Exit/Liquidity

Deal Economics - Investors want to make sure they get a big enough slice of the pie to make the investment worthwhile on a risk-adjusted basis. They want to make sure they get paid back first. They want to put a time-clock on the founders. And they want to make sure employee options don't dilute them inappropriately.

Investor Rights / Protection - Investors want to make sure no future financing deals contain terms which unduly diminish the value of their investment or lead to someone moving into a superior liquidity position (without paying appropriately for that right).

> Unless a term sheet expressly states that it contains legally binding sections, early stage investment term sheets are **not legally binding** agreements.

Governance, Management & Control - Investors want to know what's going on in the company, have a say in critical decisions, and want to protect against founder behavior that could be damaging to the company.

Exit/Liquidity - Investors want to make sure they maximize the chances to get their money back in all possible exit scenarios, even if they have to force such a situation to occur.

Fair, All Things Considered

Those goals may strike an observer as greedy (or at least aggressive) but they are not really when you consider how equity investment deals work. Unlike lenders, who have a legally-enforceable right to be repaid (often further secured by collateral or guarantees), investors purchase equity on no-recourse terms. If a company fails, the equity is worthless. Absent fraud or misdeed, equity investors have absolutely no right to be repaid. Thus investors are fully assuming the risk of failure of the venture, proportional to the amount of money they put into it. The only way they get their money back is for two things to happen in sequence:

1. The company to make progress and become more valuable and

2. An opportunity to arise in which investors can sell their stock in the company to a third party for more than their original purchase price.

In that sense, equity investment can be thought of as somewhat like a loan that the ultimate acquirer of the company is expected to repay.

Hard-Learned Lessons

Once looked at through this lens, the many provisions of a term sheet begin to make more sense and seem more reasonable. They provide protections for the many company development potholes and speed bumps experience has taught investors to expect. Whether a given term sheet represents a perfectly fair compromise is a function of the market and investing dynamics around a particular company at a particular time. Nevertheless, the term sheet negotiation process is always a constructive way to air and address the tension between investors' concerns and founders' concerns.

> Absent fraud or misdeed, equity investors have absolutely no right to be repaid. Thus investors are **fully assuming the risk** of failure of the venture, proportional to the amount of money they put into it.

powerful contractual control provisions.

- They do not want to be economically washed out by selling too much of their holdings too cheaply.
- They do not want to lose ownership of their shares if they are fired or resign.
- They do not want their company to run out of money and shut down.
- They do not want to give personal guarantees or put up their home or other assets as collateral; and
- They worry about the fit with and value-add from their investors.

Founders' Concerns

That was a quick overview of the investors' concerns, but while contemplating taking on investors in their company, founders have their own set of concerns and are worrying about a different set of issues.

- They do not want to lose control of the company, either by selling too great a percentage of their company or by agreeing to overly

The Value In The Term Sheet Process

So when investor concerns meet founder concerns, you clearly have the potential for strong tension between positions. One important role the term sheet formation process plays is to identify all the key issues and allocate the various risks between the parties. If you are successful, you will come to, and record, a negotiated middle ground on the various issues. Continue reading this book to learn how the various individual provisions work in doing exactly that.

Chapter 21

Mapping Key Deal Terms to Key Investor Concerns

In the first chapter we explain how the many concepts covered in a typical term sheet can be grouped into four main categories: Deal Economics; Investor Rights/Protection; Governance, Management & Control; and Exits/Liquidity.

Here we are going to take a first look at the individual term sheet provisions themselves and make sense of them by assigning them to the categories where they belong. We'll do this primarily from the investor perspective. In later chapters we will go deep into issues associated with each individual provision.

Deal Economics

When you think about the basic economics of a round of investment, clearly the total size of the round is a key question, as is the valuation of the company; specifically, the valuation the investor agrees to before investing. The higher the valuation, the greater the price per share, and the fewer the number of shares (and percentage of the company) will be acquired for a given investment.

A closely linked issue is the size of the option pool - investors want to invest in a company which has the tools necessary to attract and retain talent (i.e. employee stock options) and the investors want the company to establish that pool prior to their investment so that the creation of the pool does not dilute their ownership and raise the effective valuation of the deal.

This deal economics category is also where you are going to find discussion of the liquidation preference or repayment priority associated with the shares on offer. Preferred stockholders are always entitled to repayment before common stockholders, but the liquidation preference provision specifies key details: whether they are entitled to more than 1X their original money, and whether they are entitled to participate with common after they have been paid back their original principal. Liquidation preference clauses generally give the preferred holders a choice of taking their preference or converting to common. Depending on how the liquidation preference is structured, and what the exit price is, sometimes it is better to take the preference and sometimes it is better to convert to common. With participating preferred you get a bit of both - you take your original principal back and then convert and participate with common.

Dividends are the final item you sometimes see addressed in the deal economics category. It is highly unusual for a startup to agree to regular cash dividends, but accruing dividends or dividends payable in stock are often seen. Dividends function as a way to keep a time clock on the entrepreneurs to make sure there is some compensation for the passing of time.

> Depending on how the **liquidation preference** is structured, and what the exit price is, sometimes it is better to take the preference and sometimes it is better to **convert** to common.

Investor Rights/Protection

The most important topic in this category is the anti-dilution provision. This clause prevents the company from diluting investors by selling stock to someone else for a lower price than the earlier investor paid. The anti-dilution clause states that the investors' stock will be repriced downward (and they will therefore own more shares for their original investment) if stock is offered to others at a lower price. More on this complex clause later.

The anti-dilution provision is strong medicine, but indirect. The other provisions in this investor rights category attempt to control behavior more directly. The first is an assertion of the right to approve any material merger, acquisition or liquidation of the company. Because of this approval right, the transaction cannot be done without investor permission. So, the investors know they will be asked to approve a transaction in advance and can be sure they will not be surprised by a transaction after the fact.

Working in parallel are similar provisions controlling transactions involving the company's stock. The first reserves the right on behalf of investors to participate in any future financings, so that if things are going well, current investors will have the right to invest more. The second relates to secondary stock transactions - stock sold by a founder rather than by the company itself. This provision pairs two opposing sides of the same coin: a right of first refusal (ROFR) and a co-sale right. What these provisions say is that if a founder is selling any of their stock, first, the investors (or the company) will have a right of first refusal to buy that stock before it is sold to a third party. However, the investors may not want that stock, because things might not be going well, so, second, the investors pair the ROFR with an alternative right: the right to sell a proportionate amount of their own stock in any transaction that the founders are able to pull off. This way the investors are covered no matter what the transaction scenario is.

Governance, Management & Control

This category addresses the reality that investors want to know what's going on in the company, have a say in critical decisions, and want to protect against founder behavior that could be damaging to the company. Thus, the heart of this category is the right to one or more investor board seats, combined with governance provisions requiring board or committee approval for a list of important operational activities (or even in some cases reserving a veto right for the investor board member).

Paired with this in the governance category is the clause called information rights. These rights involve a requirement that the company regularly share with investors information on the company's financial and business condition.

> **Investors** want to know what's going on in the company, have a say in **critical decisions**, and want to protect against founder behavior that could be **damaging** to the company.

The final concepts in this section have to do with managing the risks associated with relying on key founders to make the company successful. The first goes under the misnomer "founder vesting". It is a misnomer because it's actually a right to claw-back some of the founder's stock in the event that the founder leaves the company in the early critical years. The right phases out over time, so it is really not vesting of ownership, it is lapsing of restrictions. Related to this is the requirement (in jurisdictions permitting it) that founders as well as other employees sign agreements not to compete with the company, use its confidential information, and/or poach its employees for a period of time following their departure.

> **Investors** want to make sure they **maximize** the chances of getting their money back in all possible **exit scenarios** (positive or negative).

Exits & Liquidity

The final category of clauses relates to the control of exits and liquidity; investors want to make sure they maximize the chances of getting their money back in all possible exit scenarios (positive or negative), even if they have to force such a situation to occur.

The key provision to accomplish that is the drag-along provision, which states that if the investors want to sell the company, and they are backed by a certain amount of stockholder support, a small minority cannot block the transaction, but must go along with the majority looking to sell.

This drag-along provision is sometimes accompanied by redemption rights, which allow investors to demand repayment of the money they invested, plus some agreed-upon return, usually during a window of time a few years out from their initial investment. If things are not going well, such a repayment could cause a cash crunch which would have the effect of forcing the company into a sale or recapitalization.

And finally, it is in the exits and liquidity section where you will see registration rights. Registration rights entitle the investors, as part of an IPO, to have their stock registered with the SEC so that they become fully liquid and tradeable after the IPO.

So that concludes a quick initial overview and mapping of the key provisions used in each of the four investor "concern categories." In the following chapters, we will dig deeper into the concepts and nuances involved in each of these provisions.

Chapter 22

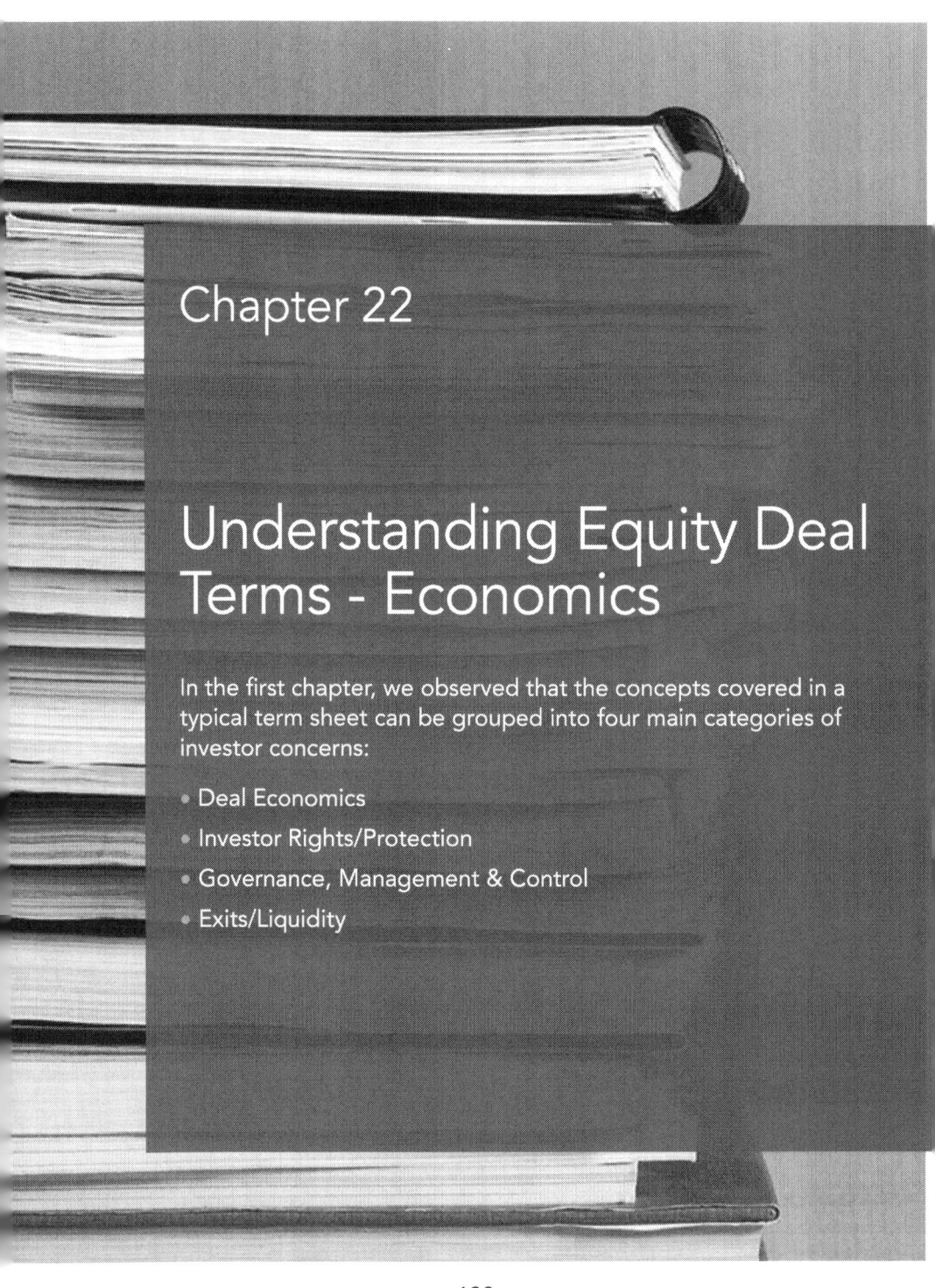

Understanding Equity Deal Terms - Economics

In the first chapter, we observed that the concepts covered in a typical term sheet can be grouped into four main categories of investor concerns:

- Deal Economics
- Investor Rights/Protection
- Governance, Management & Control
- Exits/Liquidity

In the previous chapter, we gave an overview and mapping of all of the key term sheet clauses used by investors to address the concerns in each category. In each of the next four chapters, we are going to dig deeper into the concepts and nuances involved in the provisions belonging to each category. First up are the provisions relating to Deal Economics.

Round Size

One of the first questions to be tackled is the size of the round (i.e. how much money will be invested.) Here pragmatism rules the day. Since the company's valuation is only going to go up with time and accomplishments, you always want to raise as little money as possible at today's valuation. However, there are three countervailing factors arguing in favor of doing a bigger round:

- It takes time and capital to accomplish milestones that matter,
- The future funding climate is always less certain than the present funding climate, and
- Each fund-raising event costs money and takes a great deal of founder time.

These factors amount to a solid argument for always raising a little bit more than a company thinks it absolutely needs. Things always take longer and cost more than management expects. So smart entrepreneurs and investors generally look at the key near term milestones the company needs to achieve, make a generous cost projection, and then add maybe 25% on top of that. In theory there might be a little extra dilution with this approach, but there are time and transactions savings. Nine times out of ten, the company needs the money anyway!

Valuation

Valuation is a long and therefore separate topic, but suffice it to say, it is one of the most critical aspects of any deal. It is usually set by the market (i.e. by the lead investor based on what she thinks it will take to fill the round), and that analysis is usually guided by a number of different modeling techniques and informed by experience and knowledge of her market. Future chapters in this section will talk about valuation in detail.

Option Pool Size

New investors are often puzzled by the fact that the size of the option pool is a headline issue right up there with the size of the round and the price. Shouldn't that operational detail be one of the last issues discussed? No, because the size of the option pool is closely linked to the valuation.

Investors always want the company to establish that pool prior to their investment so that the creation of the pool does not dilute their ownership and raise the effective valuation of the deal. Investors want to invest in a company which has the tools necessary to attract and retain talent (i.e.

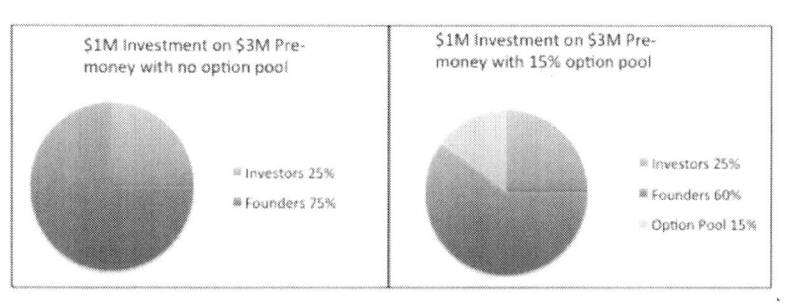

employee stock options). The bigger the pool, the bigger the tool, so investors want a good sized pool. However, since it is coming out of the pre-investment cap table, the dilutive effect for the founders is similar to a change in price. This simple chart shows a comparison of how post investment founder ownership changes with the creation of an option pool. They clearly own less of the company, but economically they should be just as well off because the company has a critical tool for growth, so the dilution should be very well spent.

$1M Investment on $3M Pre-money with no option pool
- Investors 25%
- Founders 75%

$1M Investment on $3M Pre-money with 15% option pool
- Investors 25%
- Founders 60%
- Option Pool 15%

> **Example Termsheet Option Pool Language:**
> "The total number of pre-money shares to include an unallocated employee pool large enough on a pre-money basis to equal _[10-15]_% of the total fully diluted post-money capitalization, including founders' shares, outstanding warrants and options."

Liquidation Preference

The liquidation preference is a repayment priority associated with the shares on offer. Preferred stockholders are always entitled to repayment before common stockholders, but the liquidation preference provision specifies key details like:

- Whether they are entitled to more than 1X their original money before common stock shareholders get paid, or

- Whether they are entitled to participate with common stock shareholders after they have been paid back their original principal.

Preferred always has the right to convert to common stock. If the per share price in the exit transaction is high enough, they will get a better return by converting than they will by just taking their original money back. But from time to time over the years liquidation preferences in excess of 1X have come briefly into fashion (e.g. the right to be paid 2X or 3X your original money before others are paid). That approach makes the clause into more of an offensive clause (getting a return) than a defensive clause (merely getting your principal back) and introduces financing dynamics that tend to be destructive to the company over time. This is especially true if they occur in an earlier round - all subsequent rounds want terms at least as good as earlier rounds. So, as the offensive liquidation preferences add up, the stack of money due to be paid out before founders mushrooms very quickly. If that stack gets big enough, founders have little prospect of earning a return. That can render the company unfundable because later investors don't want to invest in a company where the founders aren't going to work with all their heart because they have no reasonable expectation of return.

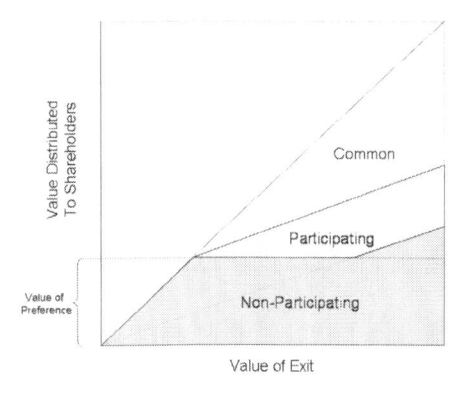

Figure 1 - Wikipedia.org

Example Termsheet Liquidation Preference Language (Participating Preferred):
"In the event of a sale, liquidation, dissolution or winding up of the Company, the proceeds shall be paid as follows: first, the original purchase price plus declared and unpaid dividends shall be paid on each share of Series Seed Stock. Thereafter, the Series Seed Stock participates with the Common Stock on an as-converted basis. A merger or consolidation (other than one in which stockholders of the Company own a majority by voting power of the outstanding shares of the surviving or acquiring corporation) and a sale, lease, transfer or other disposition of all or substantially all of the assets of the Company will be treated as a liquidation event, thereby triggering payment of the liquidation preferences described above unless the holders of a majority of the Series A Preferred elect otherwise."

One compromise in the middle is called participating preferred stock. Holders of participating preferred reserve the right to get their initial principal back first, but then also convert into common and get their share of the pay-out as a common stockholder. The reason it is a middle ground is that it is neither offensive nor defensive. This approach doesn't do much for them in a horrible outcome (where they will be lucky if there is enough to even pay some of their preference), and it doesn't really change the economics much in a grand-slam home run scenario (where the vast majority of returns is a function of the value of the common). What it does is give the holder a modest proportional sliding-scale return in a mediocre outcome. And it does so without the obnoxious, glaring, hard-coded non-linear return they'd get with a liquidation preference of greater than 1X.

The decision regarding when to take your preference and when to convert can be a tricky one, and it can be tricky to calculate the returns to common until you understand who will convert when. This cascading chain of action-consequence-reaction-consequence is sometimes referred to as a waterfall and a device called a waterfall diagram is sometimes used to graphically depict it.

Going into great detail on waterfalls is beyond the scope of this chapter, but for those who are interested, the diagram from Wikipedia.org is a simple look at a basic waterfall diagram for participating preferred. In it you can see how as exit value rises beyond various thresholds, the value available for distribution to common increases (and the incentive to convert to common kicks in).

Example Termsheet Liquidation Preference Language (Non-Participating Preferred):
"One times the Original Purchase Price plus declared but unpaid dividends on each share of Series Seed, balance of proceeds paid to Common. A merger, reorganization or similar transaction will be treated as a liquidation."

Dividends

It is very unusual for a high growth startup to pay regular cash dividends. The cash would theoretically generate a better return for shareholders if reinvested in growth and share price appreciation. But you do often see accruing dividends, which do not pay cash out in the present, but specify that they are to be paid at some future date, upon certain contingencies, or at the board's discretion. These accruing dividends can specify payment in cash, common stock or preferred stock. Aside from delivering a slightly better overall return for stockholders, these dividends serve a very useful secondary function: they keep a time clock on the entrepreneurs to make sure there is some compensation to investors for the excessive passage of time. The more time has passed, or the earlier you became a stockholder, the more your dividends amount to.

Example Termsheet Dividends Language:

"Series Seed shall be entitled to non cumulative dividends as, when and if declared. Series Seed Stock to participate in all dividends declared on an "as converted" basis. No dividends payable on Common Stock or any other Class of Preferred without payment of similar and all accrued dividends to the Series Seed Stock."

Chapter 23

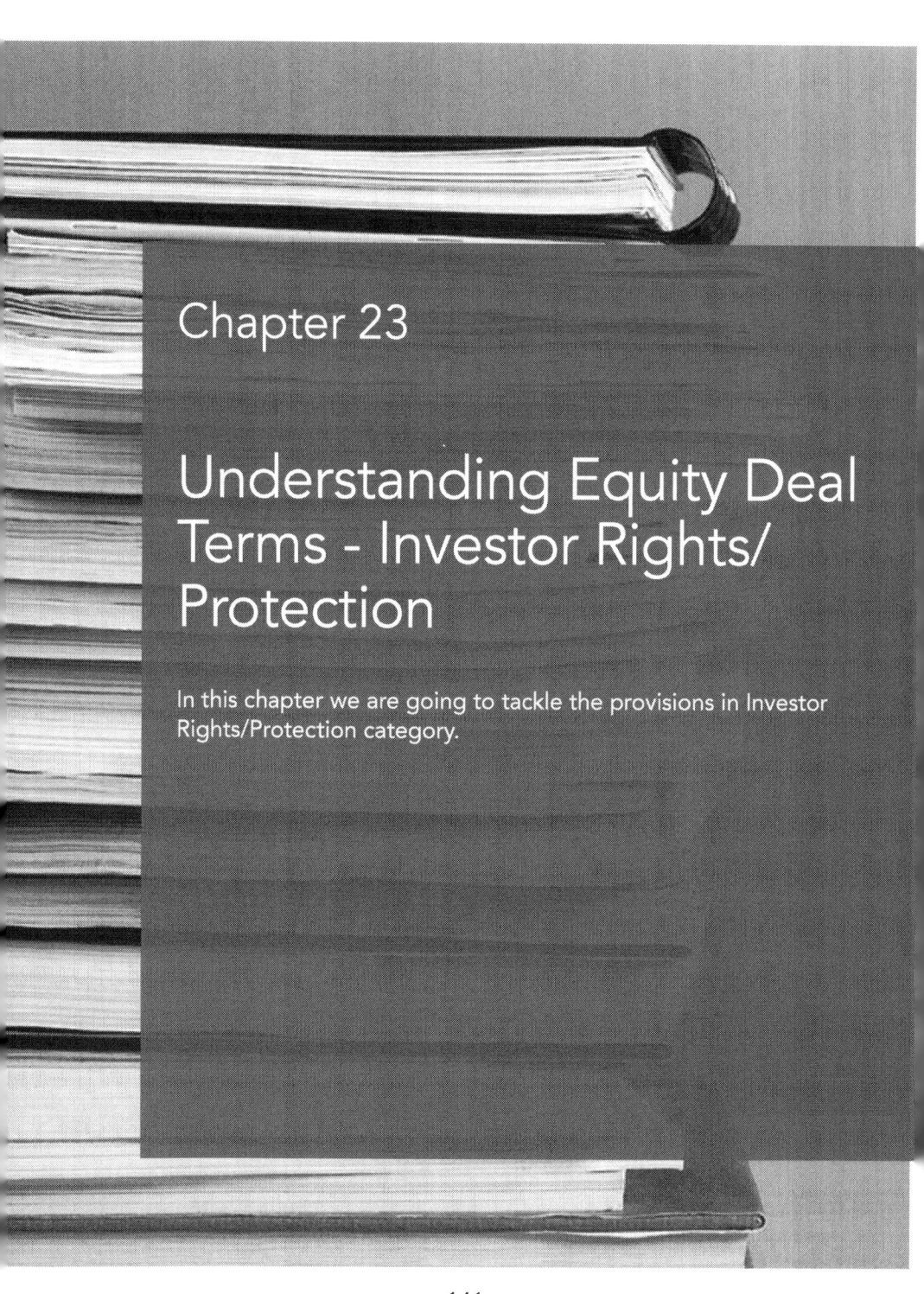

Understanding Equity Deal Terms - Investor Rights/Protection

In this chapter we are going to tackle the provisions in Investor Rights/Protection category.

Anti-Dilution

The most important provision in the protection category is the anti-dilution provision. This clause prevents the company from diluting investors by later selling stock to someone else for a lower price than the earlier investor paid. Now, it is true that any issuance of stock is technically going to be dilutive in the simplest sense of the word. This is because it will further divide the pie and lower the original investor's percentage ownership. But it is not that simple; an issuance at a higher price is merely *arithmetic* dilution rather than *economic* dilution. An investor may hold less stock, but (i) that stock has been revalued upwards by the new pricing, and (ii) the company she owns a part of also has more cash on the balance sheet. An issuance at a lower price is the opposite; it is both *economically* and *arithmetically* dilutive.

Enter the anti-dilution clause, which has almost magical properties. This clause says that if a round happens at a lower price, the earlier investors purchase price is automatically and retroactively changed, and her original investment is automatically recalculated to a lower price. In effect, she gets more stock for her original investment.

How much is the price changed? Under the terms of the rare, and unreasonably harsh, full-ratchet anti-dilution clause, all of her stock is fully repriced to the new lower price without any regard to the size (i.e. impact) of the lower-priced offering. Under the terms of the more common and more reasonable "weighted average anti-dilution clause," the size of the other offering relative to the total capitalization of the company is taken into account in the calculation. As a result, the downward adjustment of her price more closely and proportionally reflects the degree to which she was harmed. Sometimes these calculations will be broad-based. This is where the denominator for the calculation takes in every possible aspect of the company's capitalization including the option pool or as-converted common numbers after giving effect to various preferences. Sometimes it is more narrowly based and excludes things like the option pool.

Example Termsheet Anti-Dilution Language (broad-based):

"Weighted average anti-dilution, calculated as follows: in the event that the Company issues additional securities at a purchase price less than the then-current Series Seed Stock conversion price, such conversion price shall be adjusted in accordance with the following formula:

CP2 = CP1 * (A+B) / (A+C)

Where:

CP2 = Series Seed Conversion Price
CP1 = Series Seed Conversion Price in effect immediately prior to new issue
A = Number of shares of Common Stock deemed to be outstanding immediately prior to new issue (includes all shares of outstanding Common Stock, all shares of outstanding preferred stock on an as-converted basis, and all outstanding options on an as-exercised basis; and does not include any convertible securities converting into this round of financing)
B = Aggregate consideration received by the Company with respect to the new issue divided by CP1
C = Number of shares of stock issued in the subject transaction."

Full-ratchet sounds better for the investor, right? Don't be so sure. Since the economic brunt of anti-dilution clauses are felt by the founders (in the form of reduced ownership percentages), very severe anti-dilution terms can have the effect of nearly completely wiping out the holdings of the founders, thus rendering them absolutely desperate to avoid a down round at any cost. They may resort to taking any inappropriate type of investor they can find. Or if they absolutely cannot avoid a down round, they may no longer be incented to keep working for the company since they will never see a real return. So to fix that, the investors have to grant them options to keep carrying on. The net result is about as much dilution as they would have experienced with a more reasonable clause in the first place, but with a lot more work, and hard feelings, and without the flexibility of a more moderate clause.

> **Example Termsheet Control Provisions Language:**
> "So long as at least 10% of shares of the Series Seed Stock sold in this Private Placement are outstanding, in addition to any other vote or approval required under the Company's Certificate of Incorporation or By-laws, the Company will not, without the consent of the holders of at least a majority of the Series Seed Stock, either directly or indirectly by amendment, merger, consolidation, or otherwise."

Control Provisions

The anti-dilution provision is very strong medicine, but it operates automatically, indirectly, and after-the-fact. The other provisions in this category attempt to control founder behavior more directly and proactively. The first is an assertion of the right (by the board, or a class of stock, or that class' director) to approve any change of control or liquidation of the company. These clauses typically require that any merger resulting in an effective change of control of the company, any material acquisition or any liquidation of the company be approved in advance by the shareholders. Because the transaction cannot be done without investor permission, the investors know they will be asked to approve a transaction in advance and can be sure they will not be surprised by a transaction after the fact.

Other control provisions will require approval of:

- Material (i.e. significant) contracts or leases;
- Annual spending budgets and exceptions;
- Changes to the management team;
- Payment of dividends or redemptions of stock;
- Assumption of any debt obligations;

- Changes to the capitalization or authorizations of new classes of stock; or
- Changes to the charter or bylaws.

In each case the idea is investors will be at the table and have a say in any important decisions or any decisions which will affect their economic rights directly.

Pro-Rata Rights

Working in parallel are similar provisions controlling transactions not involving the company itself, but involving the company's stock. The first reserves the right on behalf of investors to participate in any future financings. If things are going well, current investors will have the right to invest more. Sometimes this right is open-ended. Other times each investor's right is capped at their pro-rata ownership in the company to allow them to maintain their percentage ownership, but no more. Thus, this clause is often referred to as "pro-rata rights."

> **Example Termsheet Pro-Rata Rights Language:**
> "Investors will have a right to maintain their pro rata interest in the Company on a fully diluted basis in any subsequent offering of securities. In any subsequent rounds of financing where the round is limited to major investors, the investments of all members [in this investor group] shall be aggregated together for the purposes of calculating whether group members count as a major investor."

Pro-rata rights can be extremely valuable rights to have in super-hot companies, so they can come with some strong provisos. In response to shenanigans where people try to profit unduly off their pro-rata rights by selling them to outsiders looking to gain access to hot deals that would otherwise be closed off, it is increasingly common to see language to ensure that the holder of pro-rata rights does not try to transfer those rights to third parties directly or indirectly through investment vehicles. Pro-rata rights may also be narrowed by calculating them without including any unexercised options or warrants a stockholder owns. Pro-rata rights for earlier shareholders may also be subject to extinguishment if they are not used each round, or they may simply be negotiated away entirely as a condition of later financing rounds.

ROFR & Co-Sale Rights

After pro-rata rights to buy more stock issued directly by the company, the second collection of protection rights in this category relates to secondary stock transactions – stock sold by a founder (or major stockholder) rather than by the company itself. This provision pairs two opposing sides of the same coin: a right of first refusal (ROFR) on one side and a co-sale right on the other. Under the terms of these provisions, if a founder or major stockholder is legally permitted to sell any of her stock, first, the investors (or the company) will have a right of first refusal to buy that stock before it can be sold to a third party. These ROFRs also generally say that if the investors don't want the stock, the company has a right to exercise the ROFR and buy it. This allows them to increase their position and keep unknown third parties out.

> **Example Termsheet ROFR & Co-Sale Rights Language:**
> "The Company will have a right of first refusal to purchase a proportional part of shares lawfully offered for sale by founders ("Founders"), management of the Company or other shareholders, if a shareholder wishes to sell stock before an initial public offering. If Investors so choose, Investors shall have the right to sell a proportional part of their holdings along with Founders or other shareholders before an initial public offering."

However, the investors may not want that stock, because things might not be going as well as hoped for the company. So, the investors pair the ROFR with an alternative right on the flip side of the coin: investors reserve the right to sell a proportionate amount of their stock as part of any transaction that the founders are able to arrange. This way the investors are covered if things are going well because they can acquire more stock and prevent new investors coming in. And, they are covered if things are going poorly because they can make sure that nobody gets liquidity before them - they get to sell a proportionate amount of their stock to any buyer who can be found.

Chapter 24

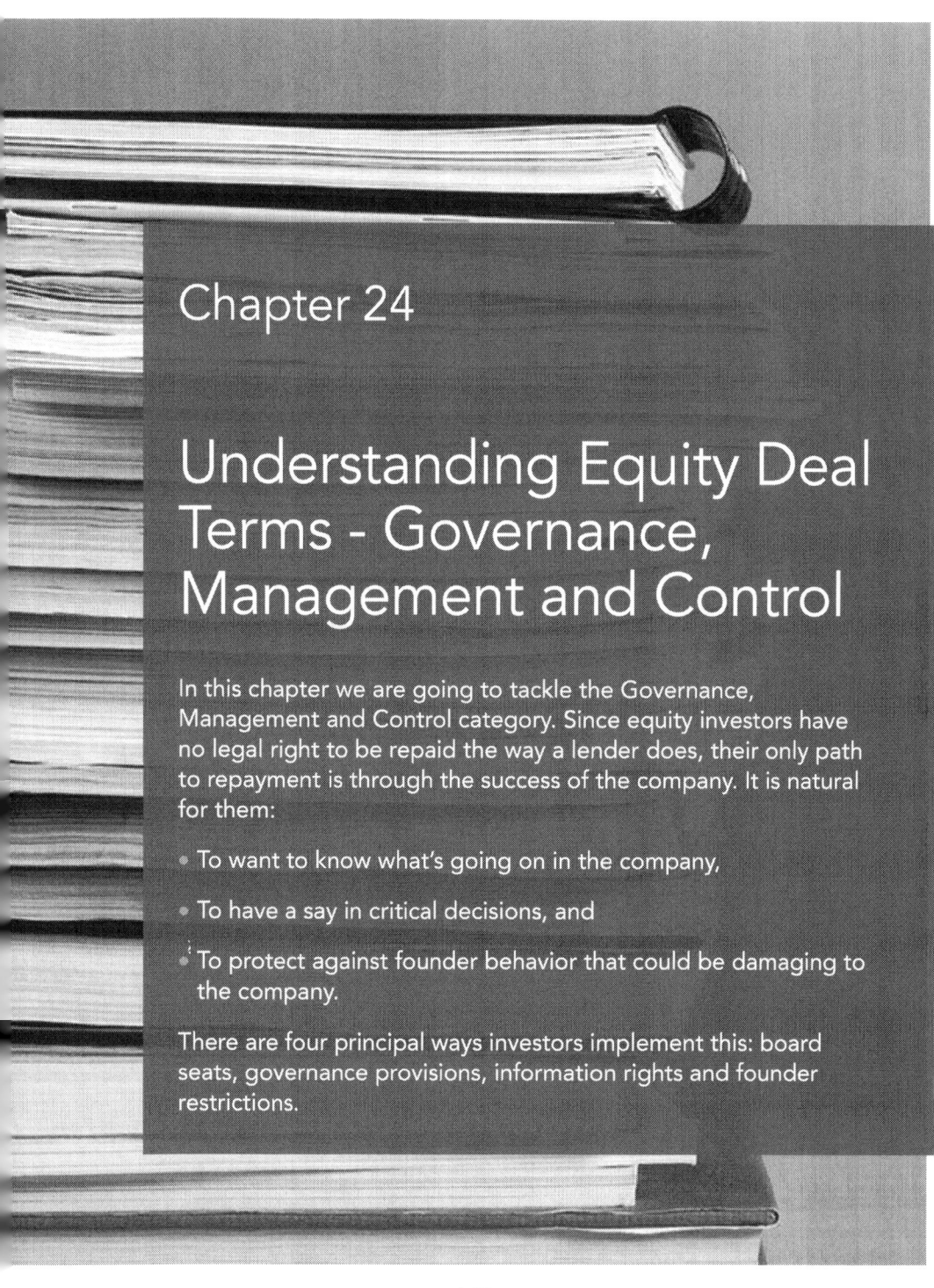

Understanding Equity Deal Terms - Governance, Management and Control

In this chapter we are going to tackle the Governance, Management and Control category. Since equity investors have no legal right to be repaid the way a lender does, their only path to repayment is through the success of the company. It is natural for them:

- To want to know what's going on in the company,
- To have a say in critical decisions, and
- To protect against founder behavior that could be damaging to the company.

There are four principal ways investors implement this: board seats, governance provisions, information rights and founder restrictions.

Investor Board Seats

The investors in a given round will typically negotiate to have a representative join the board either as a full, voting board member, or as an observer with no voting rights. In many cases they will ask for both types of seats. The board seat will typically be combined with governance provisions requiring board or committee approval for a list of important operational activities. These provisions will, in some cases, reserve a veto right for the investor board member on key matters. The investor board seat is usually not term-limited. But, the expectation and custom is that as additional investor directors are added through additional larger rounds of financing, and the board grows unwieldy, that some early investor directors may drop down to being observers, or may roll off the board entirely in the belief that it is best for the company. The right to appoint a board seat is usually part of a section which specifies the structure of the entire board.

> **Example Termsheet Board Composition Language:**
> "The Board of Directors shall initially consist of five directors and one observer:
> • the Chief Executive Officer of the Company, initially [_____]
> • a co-founder of the company, initially [_____]
> • one investor representative nominated by [lead investor] and acceptable to the holders of a majority of the Series Seed Stock (the "Series Seed Director")
> • a second investor representative nominated by the holders of Series Seed and acceptable to [lead investor]
> • an independent director nominated by the CEO and acceptable to the Series Seed Director."

Director approval rights will often cover the annual budget and any expenditures not in the budget, any borrowing, or any leases or material contracts. Stockholder approval rights will typically require a significant percentage of stockholders (or a percentage of stockholders in one class) to approve any amendments to the company's by-laws or charter in a manner adverse to the interests of preferred stockholders, any increases to the number of authorized shares of preferred stock, the authorization of any stock having equal or better rights, the redemption of any stock or payment of any dividends, or the sale, merger or liquidation of the company.

Information Rights

Paired with these board provisions are information rights, which place a requirement that the company regularly share with investors information on the company's financial and business condition. Although some CEOs will voluntarily update investors as frequently as once a month, most information rights clauses merely obligate the company to provide quarterly management reports with some financial or management dashboard data and to provide detailed annual financials, within a certain period after closing the fiscal year. With very early stage rounds, these financials are often not required to be audited. Later round investors will typically require audits. Investors also reserve the right to inspect the company's books and records, though this right is afforded them under the law of most states anyway.

Example Termsheet Information Rights Language:
"Series Seed shall have the right to the following information:
- Audited annual financial reports to Investors within 180 days of the end of the fiscal year.
- Monthly unaudited financial summary and "management dashboard" updates on progress and accomplishments against targets in past and next period, in a mutually agreeable form, to Investors by the 15th calendar day of the following month
- Annual budgets will be supplied to the Board of Directors at a regularly noticed Board meeting, but in no event later than 45 days prior to the beginning of each fiscal year for approval.

Founder Restrictions

To address the risks associated with relying on a small number of key founders to make the company successful, investors will generally insist on a couple important founder-related provisions. The first provision addresses the risk that a key founder will quit her job, leave the company with a huge gap in the team and potentially its know-how, and take a chunk of stock which will dilute the investors and potentially vote against their wishes. To prevent this, investors typically insist on what is called "founder vesting".

The term is actually a misnomer because the stock is already owned by the founder and is therefore not subject to vesting. Instead, these clauses provide for a contractual right on the part of the company to "claw-back" (buy back at a low price) some portion of the founder's stock in the event that she leaves the company in the early critical years. The right may apply to all or merely some of the founder's stock. It is always designed to phase out over time, so that more and more of the stock returns to being unrestricted each quarter or year. (Therefore it is more accurately thought of as lapsing of restrictions than vesting of ownership.)

> **Example Termsheet Founder Vesting Language:**
> "Common stock owned by any Founder with more than 5% of the outstanding, post-Private Placement equity of the Company will be subject to the right of repurchase by the Company for $0.0001 per share if the Founder's employment with the Company ceases within the first [four] years following the private placement. Such a right expires over [four] years on a monthly basis after the initial closing of the Private Placement ([2.083%] per month for 48 months)."

"Founder vesting" (i) creates a strong financial incentive to remain with the company (ii) avoids a major inequity among the founders who stayed and are working to make their stock valuable (iii) avoids dilution by pulling stock back in, which can be used to pay a hired replacement and (iv) avoids a situation where an angry departed founder controls a large voting block.

Investors will almost universally insist on clauses which forbid departed employees from using the company's confidential information for any purpose and from attempting to hire away any of its employees for a period of time following their departure. In jurisdictions where it is allowed, investors will often also require that founders as well as other employees sign agreements not to compete with the company in the event that they depart. And depending on the situation, investors will sometimes purchase one or more "key person insurance" policies to hedge the risk of death or illness of an essential founder or employee.

> **Example Termsheet Founder Non-Poaching/Non-Compete Language:**
> "In addition to standard confidentiality/assignment of inventions agreements, Founders and other key employees to execute agreements [not to compete with the Company or] solicit employees of the Company or its subsidiaries, directly or indirectly, for one year after termination of employment."

Chapter 25

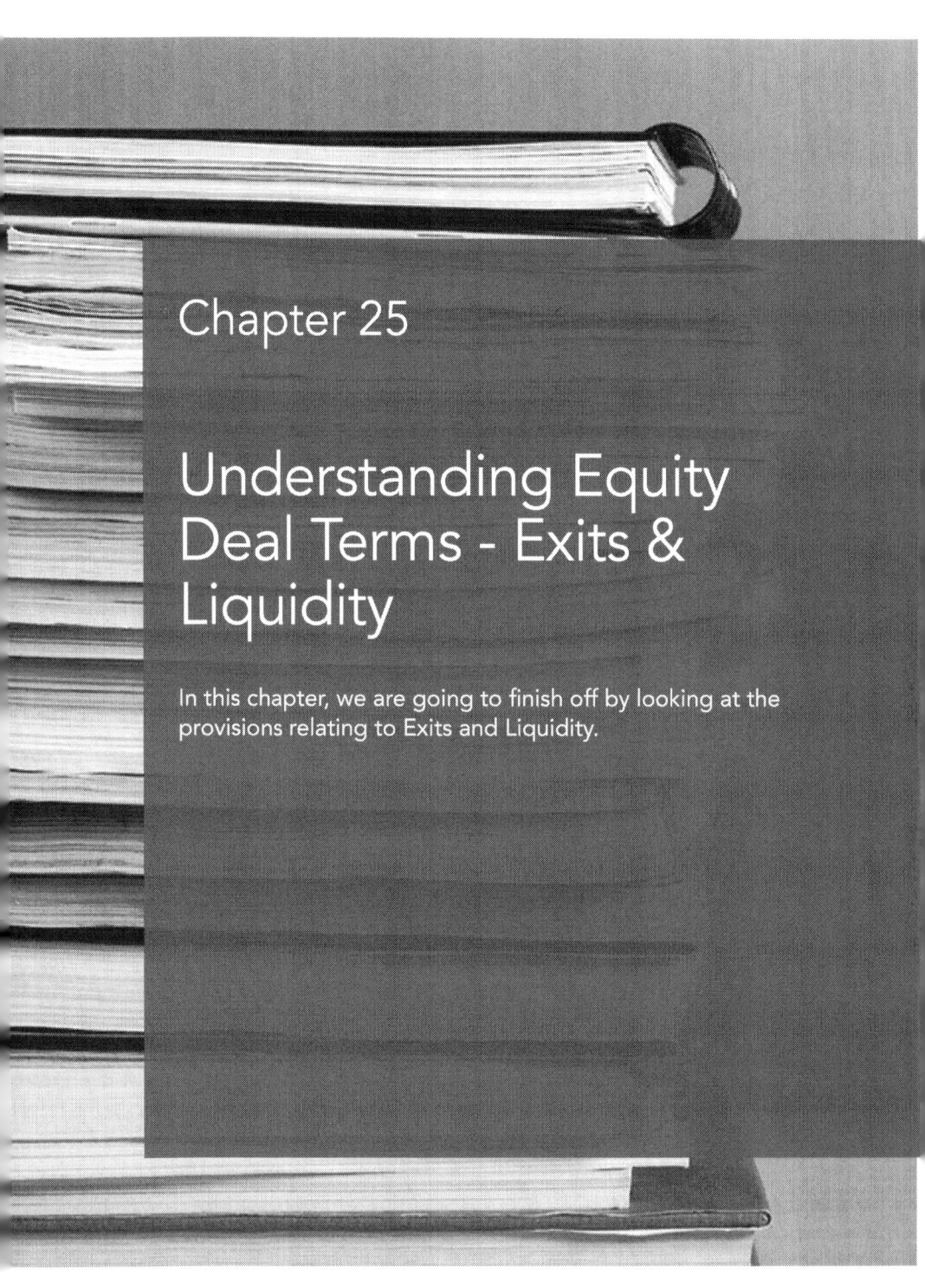

Understanding Equity Deal Terms - Exits & Liquidity

In this chapter, we are going to finish off by looking at the provisions relating to Exits and Liquidity.

Drag-Along Rights

Sometimes more euphemistically called "bring-along rights," these clauses serve a very important purpose in marginal exit scenarios. These clauses require that when a transaction amounting to a change of control of the company is proposed, and a majority of the preferred stock and a majority of the common stock are in favor of it, all stockholders have to vote in favor of it. The purpose of this should be pretty obvious: not allowing a minority of stockholders (for example, a sentimental founder, or a more optimistic and aggressive roll-the-dice investor) to block a transaction desired by a majority.

In clear-cut grand-slam scenarios this type of coercion isn't necessary. But how often do those scenarios occur? In most cases, it is much less clear whether the wiser course is to press ahead or whether to throw in the towel and sell. If you allowed group indecision to reign, nothing would ever get decided, and mediocre windows of opportunity would close, typically leaving even worse ones to follow. So even if it leads to results that are less than investors hoped, biasing things with a hair trigger toward liquidity ensures that at least investors don't waffle and end up with nothing. In effect, drag along clauses ensure that investors will make what are sometimes called type 2 errors (failing to invest in something great or in this case, selling too early) rather than the far more painful type 1 error (investing in something worthless, or in this case failing to sell something worthless when you had the chance.)

Example Termsheet Drag-Along Language:

"With respect to any transaction resulting in a "Change in Control" of the Company which transaction is approved by (i) holders of a majority of the Series Seed Stock and (ii) the holders of a majority of the Series Seed Stock and the Common Stock, voting together as a single class, all stockholders will agree to (a) vote all shares to approve such transaction, and (b) execute such other documentation and otherwise participate as is necessary to effectuate the transaction in such transaction. For purposes of these Drag Along Rights, the term "Change in Control" shall mean any sale of all or substantially all of the assets of the Company, or any sale, exchange, merger, conveyance or other disposition of securities of the Company in which more than 50% of the voting power of the Company is transferred."

Registration Rights

Registration rights address what happens with an investor's stock in the event of an IPO. IPOs are a complicated (and expensive) process that accomplish two fundamentally separate things: (i) registering the company itself as a public reporting company under the rules established by the Securities Exchange Act of 1934 and (ii) registering the stock actually being offered to the public under the rules of the Securities Act of 1933 so that the stock is freely tradeable without restriction. All investors who make it to the IPO promised land obviously want their stock to be registered and freely tradeable (so that it is not subject to holding periods and volume limitations), but the greater the number of different blocks of stock that need to be registered, the more complicated and expensive the offering is. This is especially true with secondary shares being offered by investors rather than primary shares being offered directly by the company.

> **Example Termsheet Registration Rights Language (pragmatic):**
> "The Company will covenant not to grant Registration Rights to any person or entity unless such rights also include the Series Seed Stock on a pari passu basis."

Back in the good old days (i.e. prior to about 2002), registration rights were a very important part of an early stage investment term sheet. A lot has changed since then; IPOs are a much less common method of exit for a number of reasons. So to most practitioners it seems silly to negotiate rights in a very early round that would only be used many years and many rounds of financing later, if they are even used at all. As a result, if registration rights are even included in an angel term sheet these days, they are watered down to the point of saying "we will get customary piggy-back rights" (i.e. registered secondary stock on top of the primary stock) or "if later preferred stock investors get them, we will get them on the same terms too." Footnote: if the new Reg A+ rules really catch on in a broad way and Reg A+ mini-IPOs become a common phenomenon, some new variation on registration rights might return to being a hotter topic in angel term sheets.

Redemption Rights

Another term you don't see as often in pure angel deals these days is the redemption rights clause. This clause specifies that investors have a right to demand redemption (essentially repurchase) of their stock during a specific window of time. These can be a very important tool for structured VC funds who are on a ten or twelve year time clock. This is because they allow the VC to get their money back and return it to their limited partners during the planned life of the fund. The way they do that in many cases is like a huge time bomb that creates a liquidity crisis for a fast-growing company. Management is forced to either sell the company in a non-optimized way, or stick remaining shareholders with a hasty and sub-optimal financing.

When angels do see these rights, it is usually in hybrid angel/VC rounds and they typically specify that the company will pay the redeeming party the greater of (i) fair market value or (ii) the original purchase price plus an interest rate in the 5-10% range. Redemption rights clauses can be softened in a number of ways; the opening of the window can be conditioned on certain events or set to start five or more years out, they can specify that the company has several years to get the redemption done, or that the company only has to redeem a certain fraction of the stock each year for several years.

Regardless of how they are set up, they are generally a clause that angels want to try and stay away from if they can. They do catalyze actions, but not always good ones, and often to the benefit of some stockholders over others. (For example, stock holders who cannot afford to be as patient as some investors can afford to be.)

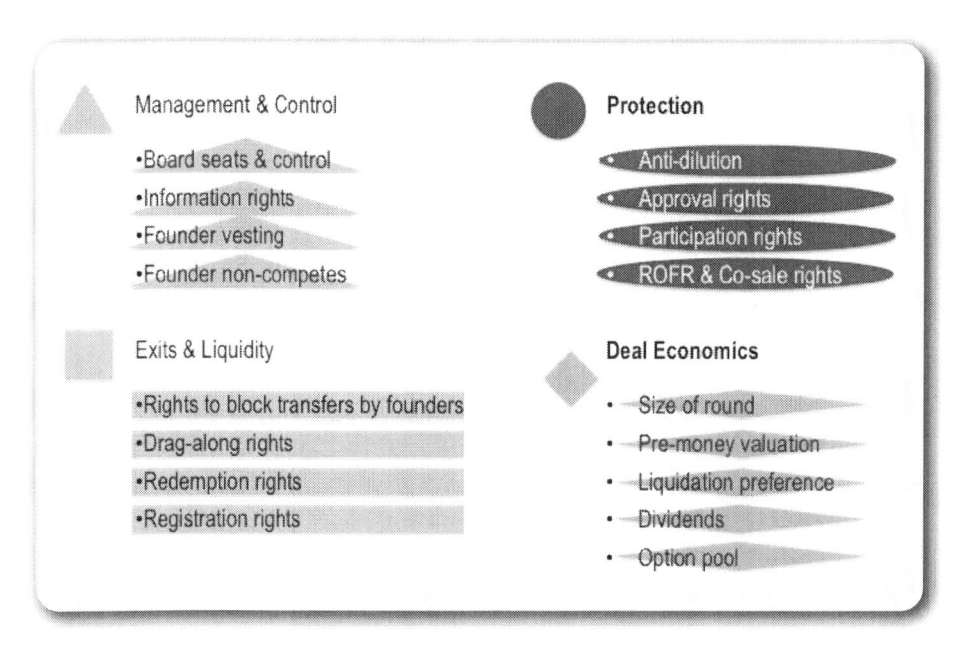

Management & Control
- Board seats & control
- Information rights
- Founder vesting
- Founder non-competes

Exits & Liquidity
- Rights to block transfers by founders
- Drag-along rights
- Redemption rights
- Registration rights

Protection
- Anti-dilution
- Approval rights
- Participation rights
- ROFR & Co-sale rights

Deal Economics
- Size of round
- Pre-money valuation
- Liquidation preference
- Dividends
- Option pool

Example Termsheet Redemption Rights Language:

"Unless prohibited by the law governing distributions to stockholders, the Series Seed shall be redeemable at the option of holders of at least [50]% of the Series Seed commencing any time after the [fifth] anniversary of the Closing, at a price equal to the Original Purchase Price plus all accrued but unpaid dividends. Redemption shall occur in [three] equal annual portions. Upon a redemption request from the holders of the required percentage of the Series Seed, all Series Seed shares shall be redeemed."

This chapter concludes our discussion on term sheets in which we talked about the main categories of investor concerns, gave an overview and mapping of all of the key term sheet clauses used by investors to address the concerns in each category, and then went back and went through each of the clauses in detail. Next we will zoom out and look at the documents these clauses are built into in order to give a more full sense of how these deals work.

Chapter 26

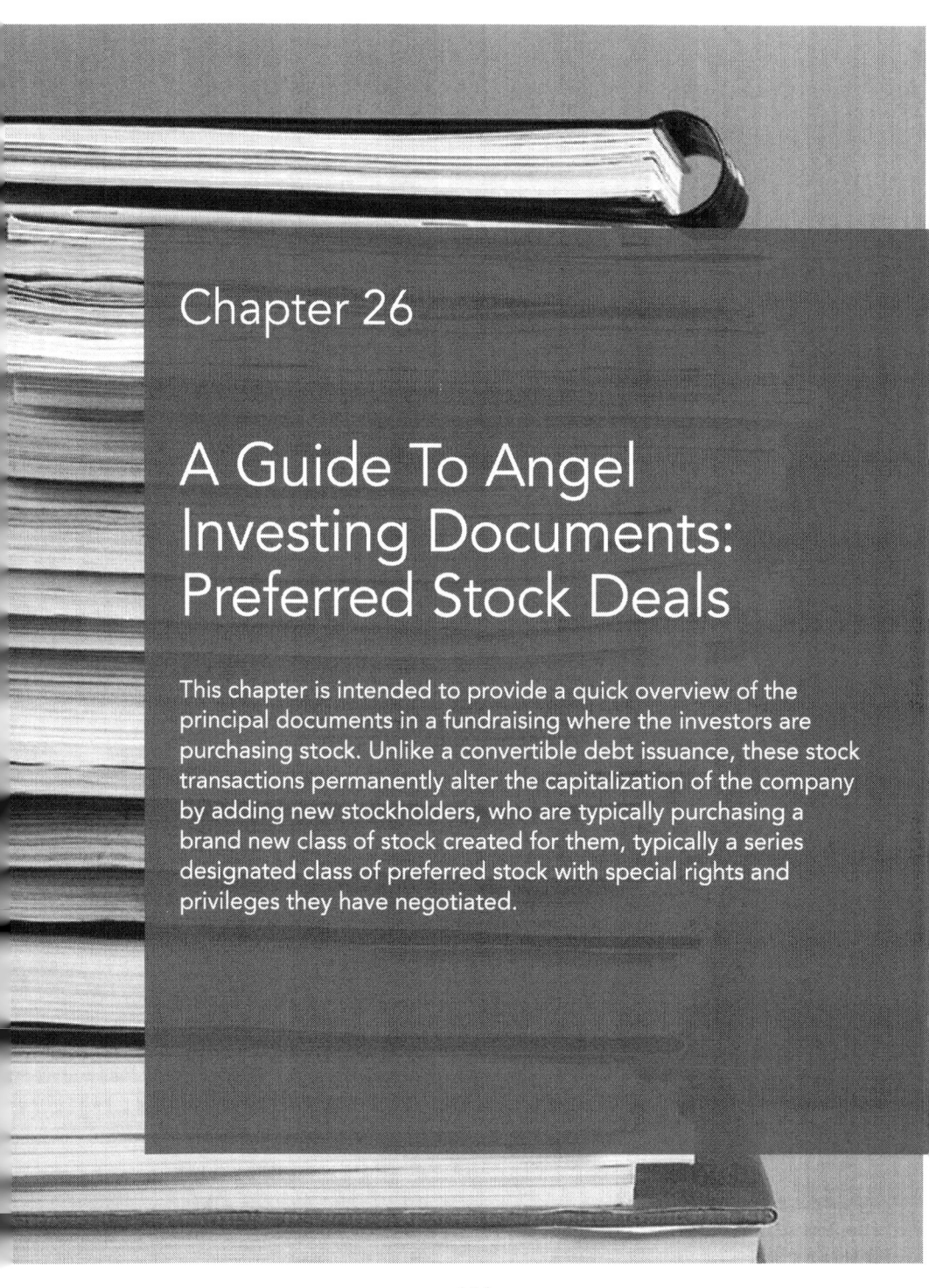

A Guide To Angel Investing Documents: Preferred Stock Deals

This chapter is intended to provide a quick overview of the principal documents in a fundraising where the investors are purchasing stock. Unlike a convertible debt issuance, these stock transactions permanently alter the capitalization of the company by adding new stockholders, who are typically purchasing a brand new class of stock created for them, typically a series designated class of preferred stock with special rights and privileges they have negotiated.

Given the permanent capitalization changes within a preferred stock deal and the associated complexity of these transactions, there are a great number of different types of deal documents used in stock transactions. For the purposes of clarity, we've divided them into Commonly Used and Occasionally Used. Readers should also keep in mind that this chapter talks in generalities. We will describe where concepts are typically covered in a given set of deal documents. Every deal is different and a given issue may be addressed by counsel in a different way or in a different document in your deal.

Commonly Used Deal Documents in Stock Transactions

Term Sheet

Most deals start with or are accompanied by a term sheet or memorandum of understanding summarizing the terms of the deal. Unless a term sheet expressly states that some or all of its sections are legally binding, early stage investment term sheets generally are not legally binding agreements. Term sheets can be thought of as a set of notes outlining the principal elements of the deal as agreed by the negotiating parties. They serve as a basis for soliciting interest from prospective investors as well as a guide for use by counsel drafting up the definitive binding documents.

Stock Purchase Agreement

The SPA is the core document of any stock transaction. Its purpose is to document and transact the sale and issuance of the actual stock, as well as to specify key terms of the deal and allocate key risks between buyer and seller.

The main sections of an SPA typically include representations and warranties by the company and the founders as to the legal and financial status of the company and its shares, the seller's right to enter into the transaction, and other important factual matters (tightly coupled with the Disclosure Schedules discussed below). There is also a section where buyers of the stock make some representations and warranties back to the seller, and a section where the buyers impose conditions which must be met before they are obligated to buy - this section often reads like a laundry list of the other transaction documents which must be in place simultaneously. And the final section is typically a long "miscellaneous" or "other matters" section containing agreements on how the SPA will be interpreted and enforced, and documentation as to agreements on other legal matters.

Disclosure Schedule (or Schedule of Exceptions)

The disclosure schedules are technically part of the SPA and work in concert with the section on company representation and warranties. Notwithstanding that, the disclosure schedule is worth mentioning separately because (i) it is invariably prepared as a separate parallel document alongside the SPA (and is typically not finalized until the last minute) and (ii) it contains key factual data and reference information about the company which may be useful to you later.

The way disclosure schedules typically work is that the SPA says in SPA section x.x: "the company has no material contracts except as listed in section x.x of the disclosure schedule" or in SPA section y.y "the company has no shares outstanding except those listed in SPA section y.y of the disclosure schedule" or in SPA section z.z "the company is not party to any litigation other than that listed in SPA section z.z of the disclosure schedule." Often when looking for reference information about a company or tracking information for your Seraf account, you can find key bits and pieces in the disclosure schedule.

Investor Rights Agreement (also sometimes Registration Rights Agreement)

The IRA is where certain rights and privileges of the new stockholders are documented. The most common rights in an IRA are (i) the right to have your stock registered with the SEC as part of an IPO, so that they are freely tradable and liquid (typically after a lock-up period of 180 days or so) and note that these registration rights are sometimes handled in a separate Registration Rights Agreement (ii) the right to receive financial and management reports and information from the company and (iii) the right to participate (i.e. purchase stock in) future financings.

IRAs sometimes also contain agreements as to the establishment and composition of board and board committees and the right of the board/committees to approve corporate budgets and extra-budgetary expenditures. IRAs can spell out the stockholder's rights with respect to dividends and sometimes IRAs contain rules for calculating share price in the event of a dilutive issuance, i.e. anti-dilution protection (though this provision is more typically found in the Certificate of Incorporation) or redemption rights which are the rights to force the company to redeem your shares for cash under certain circumstances. And finally, in some IRAs you will find language about the company's obligation to pay directors expenses and indemnify directors in the event of liability in connection with board service.

Voting Agreement

The Voting Agreement is the document used to ensure that all the signing stockholders vote in concert for the good of all. Sometimes it is just the new stockholders of one class coming in with the new round who sign the voting agreement and sometimes it is all stockholders. A voting agreement typically has provisions requiring signatories to vote to create the board structure agreed upon in the term sheet. They also typically contain what is referred to as a "drag along right" or "change of control drag along" which is the right to make the minority follow (vote for) the "will of the majority," as in approving the merger, acquisition or liquidation of the company. Often voting agreements require stockholders to vote to approve the issuance of all the new common stock necessary to convert preferred shares in the event a conversion is desirable. And typically they contain a provision stating that the stockholder automatically gives a proxy to a designate of the board to vote their shares in the event that they fail to vote them as required.

Right of First Refusal & Co-Sale Agreement

The Right of First Refusal & Co-Sale Agreement (ROFR & CSA) is a clean-up agreement used to document a couple of important rights typically included in term sheets, but not appropriate for the Stock Purchase Agreement. The first of two primary things a ROFR & CSA does is to ensure that no new shareholders are brought into the company without first giving the company the option to buy the shares proposed to be sold (instead of the proposed third party buyer) on the same terms as the proposed buyer.

ROFR & CSAs also typically state that in the event that the company does not want to buy the shares, that right goes secondarily to the existing shareholders.

The second primary thing a ROFR & CSA does is to ensure that no existing shareholders are able to exit their shares by selling to a third party without giving other shareholders the right to participate in that sale on the same terms and on a pro rata basis.

This may sound odd and contradictory, but think of it like both a floor and a ceiling: the effect of a

Stock Purchase Agreement
- Size of round
- Pre-money valuation
- Option Pool

Voting Agreement
- Drag-along rights
- Board seats & control
- Rights to block founder transfers

Investor Rights Agreement
- Registration rights
- Information rights
- ProRata / Participation
- Board seats & control
- Approval/Control rights
- Redemption rights

Certificate of Incorporation
- Anti-dilution Protection
- Liquidation Preference
- Dividends

ROFR & CoSale Agreement
- ROFR & CoSale Rights

Founder Stock Agreement
- Founder vesting
- Founder non-competes

ROFR & CSA is to ensure that (i) if things are going well with the company, existing shareholders, who took all the early risk, have first dibs on the company's shares and (ii) that if things are not going so great, nobody is allowed to find a buyer and get out unless everyone is allowed to participate in the partial liquidity event on a proportional basis.

The remainder of the ROFR & CSA is housekeeping to ensure that the mechanics of transfer are fair and smooth and any new shareholders are appropriately bound to the terms and conditions of the original shareholders.

Certificate of Incorporation or Certificate of Amendment (Articles of Incorporation in California)

It may seem odd to include a copy of state filing in a deal like this, but the reason this document is included in most early stage equity financings is fairly clever and sensible. Here's why: for most early stage financings, a new class of preferred stock is created, and the preferences or privileges of that class of stock is recorded in the company's Certificate or Articles of Incorporation. These key rights typically include liquidation preferences (getting paid before common stock or other classes of stock), dilution protection in the event of a down round, voting rights, election of directors, dividend rights, and rights relating to conversion into common stock.

What is sensible about that? Two things: (1) State law generally requires the affirmative vote of approval by the holders of a class of shares for a negative change to any of the rights of those shares, so preferred shareholders are going to have legal protection and the right to vote on any changes to their rights and privileges. For example, Delaware law says that the holders of a class must vote to approve any change which: "Increases or decreases the aggregate number of authorized shares of the affected class(es); or Adversely affects the powers, preferences, or special rights of the shares of such class." (2) Because company Certificates of Incorporation are public state filings, anyone considering purchasing the stock of a company has the right to inspect the special privileges given out to the shareholders of preferred stock and know that they are getting themselves into.

Legal Opinion

Investors buying stock in a company generally require counsel for the company to stake their reputation "vouching" for the legal status of the company and the validity of the transaction. Legal opinions in this context generally start with a recitation of all of the items counsel has reviewed prior to giving the opinion (deal documents, corporate records) and then go on to say, with varying degrees of wiggle room reserved, (i) that the company is validly existing and in good standing in the state in which it is formed, (ii) that the signing of the transaction documents is legal and accompanied by the necessary approvals and consents, (iii) exactly what the outstanding capitalization of the company is, (iv) that the issuance of the stock is legal under the relevant SEC exemptions, and (v) that there is no material litigation pending. Some things may be added and some of the wording may vary, but these are the basic things investors look for in a legal opinion.

Accredited Investor Questionnaire/ Certification

The vast majority of early stage equity financings are done pursuant to an exemption from the registration and disclosure requirements normally imposed by the US Securities and Exchange Commission on the sale of securities to the public. The scope of the exemption is rather narrow, and among other things, it requires that shares in exempt deals be sold only to accredited investors who are presumed to be sophisticated enough to evaluate a deal without public disclosure and wealthy enough to withstand a total loss stemming from an exempt deal. The accredited investor questionnaire is the document which investors fill out and sign to certify that they are accredited investors eligible to participate in an exempt offering. This questionnaire is not always a separate document - its concepts and certification are sometimes incorporated in the Stock Purchase Agreement or other deal document instead.

Signature Pages

Technically these are not a separate document in any sense of the word - typically this term merely refers to a separate electronic or paper file containing all the signature pages of all the deal documents collected together in one single document for the convenience of a signing party. Once signed, they are attached on your behalf to the relevant documents, counter-signed by the company and returned to you as part of the final closing documents package or "closing binder." Sometimes when looking for key numerical information about your shareholdings or other tracking information for your Seraf account, you can find key bits right next to your signature in the signature pages.

Occasionally Used Deal Documents in Stock Transactions

This section covers documents which turn up from time to time. It is not a problem or concern if they are not used in a given deal; it may just mean: (i) the issues to which they relate are covered in other agreements (ii) the issues to which they relate are not present or relevant in this particular deal or (iii) the lawyers drafting the deal documents have a different drafting style.

Capitalization Table

Early stage equity financings will often, but not always, include a detailed chart or table laying out all of the ownership positions of the different stockholders of the company including common stockholders, preferred stockholders and option and warrant holders (technically these last two are security holders not stockholders.) The capitalization table may either document the various positions before the close of the new round, after the close, or preferably both in one document. Often the Capitalization Table, or at least a high level summary of it, will be included in the Disclosure Schedule (above), but sometimes it is distributed as a stand-alone document. Often when looking for key numerical information about your shareholdings or other tracking information for your Seraf account, you can find key bits in the capitalization table. Capitalization tables often prove useful down the road (for example, when trying to double-check proper payouts in an exit), so it is not a bad idea to ask for a copy of the current cap table every time you invest in a company or sign deal documents. Then just upload them to Seraf with the round and you will always have them for reference.

Board Consent

A company must have the approval of its board to be authorized to partake in an equity financing. This approval is typically recorded in board minutes of a live meeting but sometimes permission is sought and recorded in writing by means of a unanimous written consent; in those cases, a copy of that written consent is sometimes included in the deal document package.

Stockholder Consent & Waiver

Similar to the board consent, under the Certificate of Incorporation or bylaws of a company an equity financing can require shareholder approval as well as board approval, so a stockholder consent is often included as part of the deal. Sometimes it is part of one of the principal deal documents, and sometimes it is a stand-alone document. If the rights of shareholders are being changed or cut back by the terms of the new deal, an explicit waiver of the abridged rights may be included to make it abundantly clear that everyone is onboard with the deal.

Irrevocable Proxy

In a typical equity deal, voting matters are left to the individual shareholders. The assumption is that it is relatively easy for a major investor to put together a majority block in favor of a proposal the major investor would like to see passed. Or a voting agreement is used. But in some deals, nothing is left to chance and investors are asked to assign their voting rights to an investor delegate (this assignment is called giving a proxy to a proxy holder) who can then vote the rights. This is a way of ensuring that shares get voted, blocks get neatly formed and no one has to spend effort or incur delay chasing votes for desirable outcomes. These proxy assignments are generally permanent and irreversible (hence the name irrevocable) transfers of voting rights, so if you see one in a deal package, read it carefully and make sure you are comfortable that the proxyholder's interests fully align with yours.

Indemnification Agreement

Although companies generally carry Directors' and Officers' insurance to protect directors from the damages and expenses of shareholder lawsuits alleging that they did something wrong as a director, many highly skilled and sought-after directors want additional protection if they are going to be convinced to serve. What companies do in that situation is offer to, in effect, re-insure the directors by indemnifying them (agreeing to reimburse them or "hold them harmless") for any expenses or damages they incur while doing their job competently and in good faith. The way this is recorded is in an indemnification clause in one of the principal deal documents, or as a stand-alone indemnification agreement. They are long and jargon-laden documents, but what they basically say is that if the director is doing a good job and acting in good faith, and they get sued by shareholders, the company will make them whole. There are a lot of details about the precise conditions in which such reimbursement will occur and the limits on that reimbursement, but if you see one of these, the concept is pretty simple - the company will cover the directors' costs.

Secretary's Certificate

The Secretary's Certificate is essentially a small cover sheet attesting to the authenticity and accuracy of the copies of the various deal approvals and governance documents. They are typically worded as a series of paragraphs each starting out with "attached is a true and correct copy of the…" and going on to list the bylaws, the board and stockholder resolutions approving the transaction, the names and titles of the current list of officers of the company and the certificates of good standing and legal existence from the state of incorporation. And they are signed by the secretary of the corporation (who may even be the CEO in small companies.)

Compliance Certificate

The compliance certificate is a belt-and-suspenders document intended to give investors extra protection by requiring the company's CEO to personally take responsibility for the transaction. Compliance certificates typically include statements that (i) all the representations and warranties the company has made in the deal documents are true, (ii) that the company has obtained all the consents, approvals, permits and waivers it needed to obtain, (iii) the shares being issued are duly authorized, and (iv) newly revised Certificate of Incorporation has been filed and is in effect. And they conclude with a simple signature from the CEO.

Joinder Agreement

Joinder agreements are sometimes used as an easy way to make new investors a party to existing agreements - they literally join you in with the other signatories. They typically list the specific agreements and their dates and make it clear that by signing the joinder agreement, the new investor is signing, and means to be bound by all the other agreements listed.

Founder Stock Agreement (aka Vesting Agreement or Restricted Share Agreement)

Term sheets in early-stage equity deals often require that the founders' stock be subject to forfeit in the event they leave the company. This concept is sometimes inaccurately nicknamed "founder vesting" but in fact what going on is that founders are agreeing to put a layer of contractual claw-back on top of stock they already own. Given this, "restrictions lapsing" is technically more correct language than "stock vesting," but the economics are equivalent. The claw-backs amount to an agreement that they will forfeit the stock (at a typically very low price so as to not cause a cash crunch for the company) if they leave. The vesting nickname stems from the fact that these restrictions lapse as time goes by. These arrangements are usually documented in agreements variously named things like Founder Stock Agreement or Vesting Agreement or Restricted Share Agreement. Investors are typically not a party to these, but a copy is sometimes furnished to them as proof of their existence because of the importance of the issue.

company has a limited operating history and may not be successful, the company has limited operating capital and might run out of money and either fail or need to raise more money on less attractive terms, competitors may out-compete the company, customers may not like the product, the company may not get sufficient intellectual property protection, the company may not be able to attract and retain enough good talent, etc. At most you will be required to acknowledge that you got your copy.

Risk Factors Statement

A list of risk factors is sometimes furnished to the investors as a way of limiting various types of liability for the company in the event that things do not go as planned or shareholders become unhappy. They literally serve as a "can't say we didn't warn you" device and work by disclosing a variety of risks associated with the investment. Example risks you might see include: the stock being offered is not registered and not liquid, the terms of your deal might be renegotiated in a later financing, the

Chapter 27

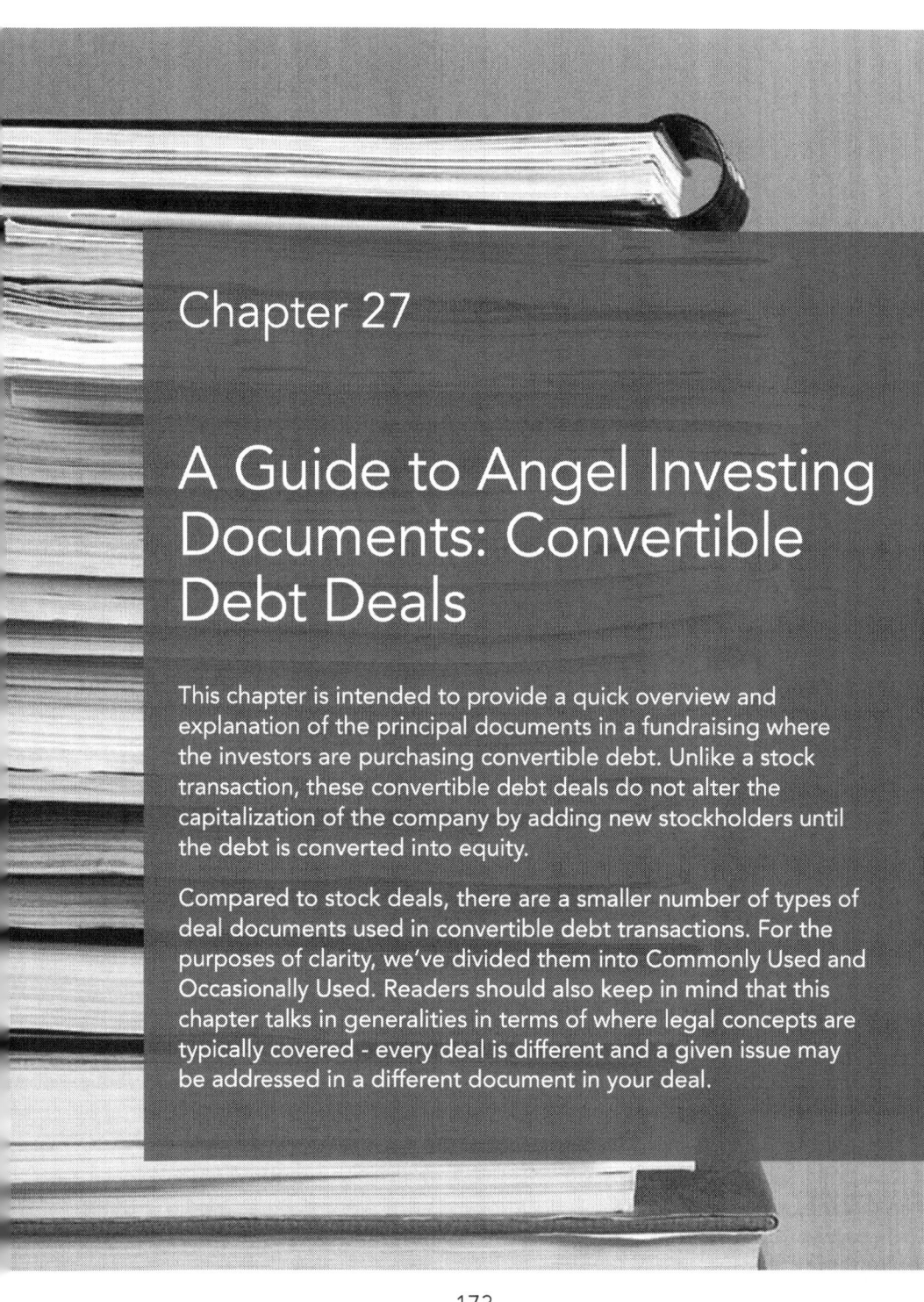

A Guide to Angel Investing Documents: Convertible Debt Deals

This chapter is intended to provide a quick overview and explanation of the principal documents in a fundraising where the investors are purchasing convertible debt. Unlike a stock transaction, these convertible debt deals do not alter the capitalization of the company by adding new stockholders until the debt is converted into equity.

Compared to stock deals, there are a smaller number of types of deal documents used in convertible debt transactions. For the purposes of clarity, we've divided them into Commonly Used and Occasionally Used. Readers should also keep in mind that this chapter talks in generalities in terms of where legal concepts are typically covered - every deal is different and a given issue may be addressed in a different document in your deal.

Commonly Used Deal Documents in Convertible Debt Deals

Promissory Note

The Promissory Note (or Convertible Promissory Note) is the actual debt instrument in the deal. In reality it is nothing more than a fancy I.O.U. It states the names of the lender and borrower, the date of the debt, the amount of indebtedness, the interest rate, the interest rate calculation mechanism (annual, semi-annual, cumulative, non-cumulative) and the maturity date (due date). Then, usually immediately after those terms there will be some discussion of any negotiated cap on the conversion price or discount against the conversion price if the deal features a cap or discount.

The rest of the note is typically dedicated to setting out the mechanics of converting the debt repayment into stock. In this section you will find language outlining what constitutes a qualified financing - a note-holder does not want stock in a company that is underfunded (she would rather have a cash repayment), so the concept here is to say that "it needs to be part of a pretty robust financing if you are going to convert me into stock." There is also typically some language about what happens if there is no qualified financing before the maturity date. And the final few paragraphs are the usual legal housekeeping clauses about contractual interpretation and enforcement.

Special Terms: Subordination, Security Interests and Guarantees - Occasionally notes will incorporate the concept of subordination, security interests or guarantees. These features are more typical of classic bank type debt, and less common in investor convertible debt, but they are worth mentioning because they do show up occasionally.

- **Subordination** is a legal concept where a lender agrees that its right to receive repayment is subordinate to (i.e. in a lower position or in second priority to) another lender's right to repayment. For example, most banks who have lent to a company will immediately recall their loan if the company tries to borrow from investors unless investors agree their debt is subordinate to the bank's debt.

- **Security Interests** are legal rights allowing the lender to more easily seize collateral in the event of a default on the loan. A note that includes a security interest is called a secured note. These security interests require additional public record state filings to perfect and they are typically signaled in the title of the instrument (e.g. Convertible Secured Note) or right near the beginning of the text.

- **Guarantees** are personal undertakings by someone involved in a corporation to repay the corporation's debt if the corporation fails or defaults on the debt. Banks typically insist on personal guarantees from CEOs before lending, and they may take a security interest in the CEO's home or some other major asset as collateral. Personal guarantees are not common with straight investor debt and probably best avoided - either you believe enough in the CEO and the concept to invest and assume the risk of failure, or you don't.

Occasionally Used Deal Documents in Convertible Debt Deals

Note Purchase Agreement

A Note Purchase Agreement (sometimes called a Subscription Agreement - see below) is a contractual wrapper that makes a note financing a little bit more formal and a little bit more like a stock financing. It typically outlines the mechanics of the closing (to make sure no individual note holders get caught out as the only ones investing), it adds in some representations and warranties on the part of the company around validity and authorization, it add some note holders reps and warranties around eligibility as an accredited investor, and in some rare cases, it may serve to cover some of the key provisions you might expect to see in a Note Holders Agreement or a Voting Agreement (both discussed below.)

Subscription Agreement

A note Subscription Agreement is very similar to a Note Purchase Agreement (above) - mostly it is just a naming convention. Occasionally, however, you will see subscription agreements used to take some of the more complex terms of a note out of the note itself and into a separate subscription contract such that the note and the subscription agreement work as two halves of one convertible debt deal. The effect of doing it this way is the same, it just allows for a more simple note and a more thorough treatment of conversion mechanics in a more traditional contract format.

Note Holders Agreements and Voting Agreements

Sometimes the holders of a note will wisely insist on things like board seats, information rights, covenants against issuing stock or other debt and/or other terms more typically associated with stock deals. When this happens, these contractual agreements between the company and the noteholders are usually written up in a separate agreement given a title like Note Holders' Agreement or Voting Agreement.

Subordination Agreement

Sometimes subordination of debt (see above) is done by means of a stand-alone agreement. This most often occurs when new debt is added after the debt to be subordinated is already in place - for example when there is an outstanding convertible debt round and a revolving line of credit from a bank is added, and the parties enter into a new agreement to make it clear that the old debt is subordinate to the new debt.

Warrant to Purchase Stock

One of the complaints about convertible notes in the early stage context is that they amount to equity risk for debt returns. This results in pricing incentives that lead to a misalignment of interests between company management and the investors. People try to address this with the terms of the note - for example caps on the conversion price and discounts on the conversion price. But these mechanisms do not fully align the interests of the founders and the note holders, so in an effort to better address that, sometimes warrants to purchase shares are given in lieu of or in addition to caps and discounts. It obviously makes the note perform economically more like equity since warrants literally are securities derived from equity, but warrants do introduce a bit of complexity into what is supposed to be a simple transaction.

This book is brought to you by the founders of **Seraf**. Seraf is a web-based portfolio management tool for investors in early stage companies. Seraf's intuitive dashboard gives angel investors the power to organize all of their angel activities in one online workspace. With Seraf, investors can see the combined value of their holdings, monitor company progress, analyze key performance metrics, track tax issues, store investment documents in a cloud-based digital locker, and more. Seraf's easy interface enables investors to track their angel portfolios as efficiently as they track their public investments. To learn more, visit **Seraf-Investor.com**.

Hambleton Lord is Co-Founder of Seraf and the Co-Managing Director of Launchpad Venture Group, an angel investment group focused on seed and early-stage investments in technology-oriented companies. Ham has built a personal portfolio of more than 35 early stage investments and is a board member, advisor and mentor to numerous start-ups.

Seraf Co-Founder **Christopher Mirabile** is the Chair of the Angel Capital Association and also Co-Managing Director of Launchpad Venture Group. He has personally invested in over 50 start-up companies and is a limited partner in four specialized angel funds. Christopher is a frequent panelist and speaker on entrepreneurship and angel-related topics and serves as an adjunct lecturer in Entrepreneurship in the MBA program at Babson. Due to their combination of roles as investors, advisors and angel group leaders, Ham and Christopher were named among Xconomy's "Top Angel Investors in New England."

Printed in Great Britain
by Amazon